KINGDOM BIBLE STUDY SERIES

KINGDOM BIBLE STUDY

VOLUME 1: The Comprehensive Guide to Christian Salvation

Written by Pastor John Michael Stewart
(Revised November 17, 2022)

Copyright © 2020 Written by Pastor John Michael Stewart
All rights reserved.
ISBN: 9798634091488

Stephen Johnson, Graphic Designer
Stephen's Creative Design
www.stephenscreativedesign.com

Valesa Clouse, Publishing Format
cValesa Instructional Design
contact@cvalesa.com

KINGDOM BIBLE STUDY SERIES

TABLE OF CONTENTS

INTRODUCTION   v
    Purpose of the Kingdom Bible Study

LESSON 1: REPENTANCE   1
Topics:
    What the Word Says About Sin
    The Purpose of Repentance
    How to Stop Sin
    Frequency of Sin
    How and Why Sin Can Occur

LESSON 2: BAPTISM   13
Topics:
    What the Scripture Says About Baptism
    The Purpose of Baptism
    Baptism and Salvation
    The Requirements of Baptism
    Types and Shadows of Baptism

LESSON 3: HOLY GHOST   22
Topics:
    What the Scripture Says About the Holy Ghost
    The Purpose of the Holy Ghost
    Spiritual Gifts
    Speaking with Tongues
    Four Types of Tongues
    Who Speaks in Tongues
    What is Edification
    Why Speaking with Tongues
    Tongues and the Devil
    Speaking with Tongues Today

LESSON 4: WALKING IN THE SPIRIT   40
Topics:
    What the Scripture Says About Walking in the Spirit
    The Purpose of Walking in the Spirit
    Faithfulness, Bible Reading

  Prayer, Group Bible Studies
  Mentorship/Discipleship, Obedience
  Separation, Witnessing
  Fasting, Giving/Tithes

LESSON 5: TRUTH (Part 1)   48
Topics:
  What the Scripture Says About Truth
  The Purpose of Truth
  The Revelation of Truth
  The History of Christian Doctrine

LESSON 6: TRUTH (Part 2)   Presenting Truth to the Masses   61
Topics:
  What Is Believing, Faith, and Works
  The Modern-Day Christian Salvation Message
  Taking Every Bible Verse Literally
  Accepting Apostolic Truth
  The Product of False Teaching

LESSON 7: Wise as a Serpent and Harmless as a Dove   91
Topics:
  For Teachers Only
  Know Your Material
  Dealing with Resistance
  Dealing with Rejection
  Having the Right Spirit
  Do No Harm
  Know When to Move on
  How to be the Most Productive

FINAL CONCLUSION   95
Topics:
  Trust the Word
  Follow the Word
  Teach the Word
  Be Prepared
  Be Ready for Revival

INTRODUCTION

The Kingdom Bible Study (KBS) provides the most significant scriptures in the Word of God for the most important topics relevant to a person's spiritual maturation. I call these scriptures "hammer down" scriptures because they are so clear and concise. The lessons included in this Bible study will introduce a person to exactly what is required to get saved and stay saved. When a spiritual foundation has been established, the KBS is an amazing tool for the student to become the teacher.

The Bible makes it very clear that there is an expectation from God to become a laborer for Him and to bring in His harvest. *Matthew 9:37 Then saith he unto his disciples,* ***The harvest truly is plenteous****, but the labourers are few;* ***38 Pray ye therefore the Lord of the harvest, that he will send forth labourers into his harvest.*** The KBS is designed to create that laborer in you! TEACHERS: Don't teach any lessons to anyone until you have read Lesson 7.

We are considered slothful and evil servants if we do not increase God's kingdom. *Matthew 25:24 Then he which had received the one talent came and said, Lord, I knew thee that thou art an hard man, reaping where thou hast not sown, and gathering where thou hast not strawed:25 And I was afraid, and went and hid thy talent in the earth: lo, there thou hast that is thine. 26 His lord answered and said unto him,* ***Thou wicked and slothful servant, thou knewest that I reap where I sowed not, and gather where I have not strawed: 27 Thou oughtest therefore to have put my money to the exchangers, and then at my coming I should have received mine own with usury.*** *28 Take therefore the talent from him, and give it unto him which hath ten talents. 29 For unto every one that hath shall be given, and he shall have abundance: but from him that hath not shall be taken away even that which he hath.* ***30 And cast ye the unprofitable servant into outer darkness: there shall be weeping and gnashing of teeth****. To increase the Kingdom, we must bring people to the understanding of who Jesus is and what He wants us to do. The way we do that is through witnessing and teaching Bible studies. The consequence of not doing these things is to be cast into darkness where there is weeping and gnashing of teeth.* We all know where that is! We do NOT have to suffer that fate!

While teaching these lessons the more inexperienced teacher may stick to this study, point by point. Those that have more experience, are sure to be inspired to add their own experiences and knowledge. To them, this will be a simple guide to direct their students in Bible study. With the KBS, you have everything you need to participate in the most important and gratifying task from God: to reach the lost and teach them how to get out of the darkness and into His glorious light. *Colossians 1:27 To whom God would make known what is the riches of the glory of this mystery among the Gentiles; which is Christ in you, the hope of glory: 28 Whom we preach, warning every man, and teaching every man in all wisdom; that we may present every man perfect in Christ Jesus:*

Note to teacher: These lessons are in-depth and are not designed to be taught in one session.

KINGDOM BIBLE STUDY SERIES

Lesson 1
REPENTANCE

Most people do not understand the biblical meaning or definition of repentance, even if they have been in church for an extended period of time. If asked, most people would reply by saying: a) to say I'm sorry for my sin, and/or b) to ask for forgiveness. However, these are only two out of the three parts of repentance. The third part is the most important. Repentance can be defined as God's request for us to STOP sinning! Another way to say it is to TURN AWAY from sin and RUN toward Jesus!

How does sin happen? Is it automatic? The answer is NO; sin is a choice. We can choose to sin or not, that is up to the individual. There is a way to stop sin, and we learn exactly how to do so in the book of Galatians. ***Galatians 5:16 This I say then, walk in the Spirit, and ye shall not fulfil the lust of the flesh.*** *25 If we live in the Spirit, let us also walk in the Spirit.* If we follow the instructions given in the Word of God, it will lead us into a spiritual life full of the Holy Ghost. Then, we will be able to STOP sin in our lives through the power of the Holy Ghost. *Acts 1:8 But ye shall receive power, after that the Holy Ghost is come upon you: and ye shall be witnesses unto me both in Jerusalem, and in all Judaea, and in Samaria, and unto the uttermost part of the earth.*

The following scriptures will give us a deeper understanding of repentance.

1. **Luke 13:3 I tell you, nay: but, except ye repent, ye shall all likewise perish.**
   Luke 13:5 I tell you, nay: but, except ye repent, ye shall all likewise perish.

   - Jesus spoke of the people in Siloam who had a tower fall on them and it killed them. He was saying that without repentance a person will die a spiritual death.

   - The level or magnitude of sin is irrelevant. The fact is that everyone needs to repent, or they will perish.

2. **Luke 24:47 And that repentance and remission of sins should be preached in his name** among all nations, beginning at Jerusalem.

   - Repentance (and baptism), is to be taught to everyone, everywhere. Everyone needs to turn from sin, and everyone needs baptism.

   - Everyone is required to repent to be saved. No exceptions.

3. Mark 1:15 And saying, the time is fulfilled, and the kingdom of God is at hand: **repent ye, and believe** the gospel.

- The time is now to repent, not later. If you don't repent, do you really believe the gospel? The answer is no!

- Repentance and believing are connected. You cannot be a believer if you don't repent of your sins.

4. Acts 2:38 Then Peter said unto them, **Repent**, and be baptized every one of you in the name of Jesus Christ for the remission of sins, and ye shall receive the gift of the Holy Ghost.

- This is the God-given salvation equation, delivered by the apostle Peter. The first step leading to salvation is **Repentance**.
- Repent means to do an about-face, or a 180° turn, not a 360° turn. If you do a 360°, you'll end up in the same sinful state you started in.

- Before Christ, you're heading toward the devil and Hell. After Christ, you do a 180° and are now heading toward Jesus.

- No one is perfect. The only thing we can do perfectly is repent. If you sin again after your initial repentance, then you must repent again!

5. 2 Corinthians 7:9 Now I rejoice, not that ye were made sorry, but that ye sorrowed to **repentance:** for ye were made sorry after a godly manner, that ye might receive damage by us in nothing.

6. 2 Corinthians 7:10 For godly sorrow worketh **repentance** to salvation not to be repented of: but the sorrow of the world worketh death.

- These two scriptures simply say that the apostle Paul found no joy when people went through trials and tribulations. But if those tough times bring people to repentance, that would bring him joy.

- There is a sorrow of the world, which is to say sorry and continue to sin. There is also a godly sorrow, which is to say sorry and then stop doing the sinful behavior.

- Verse 10 tells us once you have repented of sin; you are not supposed to go back to that sin. That is what it means to say, "not to be repented of." It states clearly that repentance leads to salvation.

- The goal in life for every Believer-Christian-Saint of God, should be to live a REPENTED life. This means you fight to make sure that you don't sin, every day! If you fall short and sin, repent and go back to fighting sin daily.

7. **Hebrews 12:17** For ye know how that afterward, when he would have inherited the blessing, he was rejected: for he found no place of **repentance,** though he sought it carefully with tears.

- Just because a person cries and weeps in the middle of their troubles or at the church altar, does not necessarily mean that the person is repented.

- God hated Esau because he would not repent, even after the shedding of tears. Esau did not get the inheritance of the blessing, (**Romans 9:13, Malachi 1:3**).

- If a person does not repent, they will not get the inheritance that Jesus has in store for them. That inheritance is salvation.

I. "I AM A SINNER AND I SIN EVERY DAY"

- This is a very common teaching in today's Modern Christianity. But the scripture, simply does not support such ideas.

- For a person who has been in church for a while, and say that they sin every day, is like a person who is 25 years old, and perfectly healthy, and says they are still in diapers. Something would be very wrong with that.

8. **Romans 6:1** What shall we say then? **Shall we continue in sin, that grace may abound? 2 God forbid.** How shall we, that are dead to sin, live any longer therein? 15 What then? shall we sin, because we are not under the law, but under grace? God forbid.

- This entire chapter of Romans 6 states that we are to live free from sin 16 times. God makes it very clear that sin is not to be a daily occurrence.

- There is no question what God expects from us.

Lesson 1 REPENTANCE

II. "IS SIN A REGULAR OCCURRENCE IN A CHRISTIAN'S LIFE?"

9. **Isaiah 59:1** Behold, the LORD'S hand is not shortened, that it cannot save; neither his ear heavy, that it cannot hear: 2 **But your iniquities have separated between you and your God**, and your sins have hid his face from you, that he will not hear.

    - Sin separates us from the Lord, and His salvation, until a person repents.

    - If people want to continue in sin, God will not hear their prayers, and intimacy with God will be impossible.

10. **James 4:4** Ye adulterers and adulteresses, know ye not that the friendship of the world is enmity with God? whosoever therefore will be **a friend of the world is the enemy of God.**

    - A person can't be in sin and still be in the Kingdom. **1 Corinthians 10: 21** Ye cannot drink the cup of the Lord, and the cup of devils: **ye cannot be partakers of the Lord's table, and of the table of devils.**

    - Therefore, the Bible emphasizes repentance. God does not want to be our enemy. He loves us and wants us to be saved. (*John 3:16*)

11. **1 Corinthians 6:9** Know ye not that the unrighteous shall not inherit the kingdom of God? Be not deceived: neither fornicators, nor idolaters, nor adulterers, nor effeminate, nor abusers of themselves with mankind, 10 Nor thieves, nor covetous, nor drunkards, nor revilers, nor extortioners, **shall inherit the kingdom of God.** 11 And such **were some of you**: but ye are washed, but ye are sanctified, but ye are justified in the name of the Lord Jesus, and by the Spirit of our God.

    - The Bible says that people who are in sin cannot go to Heaven!

    - Then the Bible clarifies that the church in Corinth **"were"** sinners, past tense. Which means, they had an encounter with God, and as a result of that encounter, the people in the church of Corinth repented.

    - This is what Jesus wants from us today; to have an encounter with Him, and that encounter should lead us to repentance.

12. **Galatians 5:16** This I say then, Walk in the Spirit, and ye shall not fulfill the lust of the flesh.

    - If a person does the things the scripture tells us to do, then people will be full of the Spirit. As a result, people WILL NOT sin.

- If a person doesn't walk in the Spirit, they will most certainly sin.

- This concept is what makes sinning a choice. If you choose not to be spiritually strong, then you're choosing to sin.

- The idea of walking in the Spirit is so important, that the entire 4th lesson of the KBS is dedicated to the subject. It might be one of the most important Bible studies there are.

13. **Galatians 5:21** Envyings, murders, drunkenness, revellings, and such like: of the which I tell you before, as I have also told you in time past, that **they which do such things shall not inherit the kingdom of God**.

- There is a consequence for living in sin. It is not having the ability to go to Heaven.

- Jesus gives us a way out of sin. That is repentance. When we sin, we are despising God. Repentance is how we reconnect with God after we sin.

14. **James 1:21** Wherefore lay apart all filthiness and superfluity of naughtiness, and **receive with meekness the engrafted word**, which is able to save your souls. **22 But be ye doers of the word, and not hearers only, deceiving your own selves.**

- This is a call for the church to receive the Word and turn from sin.

- When we repent, it is a part of our salvation. We are saved by *doing* what the Word of God says, and not just *hearing* it in church and during Bible studies.

- If we are not taking action to obey the Word of God, and we believe we are still ok with God, then we are fooling ourselves.

15. **1 Corinthians 10:13** There hath no temptation taken you but such as is common to man: but God is faithful, who will not suffer you to be tempted above that ye are able; but will **with the temptation also make a way to escape**, that ye may be able to bear it.

- Jesus can ask us to live free of sin because he always gives us a way to escape sin. Just because life gets rough, does not give us an excuse to sin.

- God will not allow you to be tempted beyond what you are able to bear. So, if you're going through it, God knows you can handle it.

- If a person sins as a result of a trial in their life, it means the person gave up before the miracle could happen. To overcome sin is to bring purpose to your pain.

- How? Because when you overcome something, God is going to send people to you that need to overcome the same issue you had. Now you will have the experience you need to help them overcome, as well.

16. **1 John 1:6** If we say that we have fellowship with him, and walk in darkness, we lie, and do not the truth:7 But if we walk in the light, as he is in the light, we have fellowship one with another, and the blood of Jesus Christ his Son cleanseth us from all sin. **8 If we say that we have no sin, we deceive ourselves, and the truth is not in us**. 9 If we confess our sins, he is faithful and just to forgive us our sins, and to cleanse us from all unrighteousness. **10 If we say that we have not sinned, we make him liar, and his word is not in us.**

- We cannot claim fellowship with God and be in sin at the same time. *(Romans 8:6-9)*.

- If we are walking in the light, then we obey the scriptures. When we have the light, we have fellowship with Jesus.

- 1John is written to the church, which was established on the **Acts 2:38** salvation message. It is not describing how to get saved. It is speaking to people who have already entered into salvation.

- Verse 8 is often taken out of context and has been translated by some to say that we have daily, regular, perpetual sin in our lives as a born-again Christian.

- However, verses 6 and 9 put verse 8 in context. Verse 6 already negates sin as an acceptable part of Christian life. Verse 9 demonstrates that when you confess sin, it will lead to God's forgiveness. Your sins will be forgiven when you repent.

- Then Verse 9 states that we will be cleansed by the blood from all unrighteousness. The Bible is clear, one repents first for the forgiveness of sin, then the cleansing takes place when you are water baptized (*See Lesson 2: Baptism*).

- Some teach from verse 9, that confession or fellowship, brings the washing away of sin. That is impossible and is a contradiction to the Word of God. In Lesson 2, we will learn unequivocally that Baptism is the mechanism in which sins are washed away. There are not two ways to wash away sins in the Bible.

- Even without using the specific word, Baptism, this verse is describing how a person is cleansed of unrighteousness by the blood in Baptism.

- Verse 10 shows, that the verse is referring to past sin, by the past tense usage of the words "have not sinned". Verse 8 says that a person is untruthful if they say they have no sin. Verse 10 says, we make God a liar if we say we have not sinned, sometime in our lives, and God's Word is not in us.

- Since Verse 10 is talking about past sins, verse 8 also appears to be talking about past sins. So, we are NOT a liar if we say that we have had past sins that we repented of. We are NOT a liar if we say we have stopped those past sins.

- The fact remains, saying that we have sin on a daily or regular, consistent basis, as a Christian, is NOT consistent with the rest of scripture.

- These passages are NOT stating that a born-again Christian seeking or proclaiming they are free of sin, in the present, makes them a liar.

- These passages ARE stating that if a person suggests that they don't have any past sins, so they don't need God's forgiveness and cleansing, then they are a liar, and the truth is not in them.

17. **1 John 2:1** My little children, these things write I unto you, **that ye sin not.** And if any man sin, we have an advocate with the Father, Jesus Christ the righteous:

    - This is the call of God. DO NOT SIN!!! The Word also tells us if we do sin, the mercy of God gives us someone to turn to. If we sin, we must turn to Jesus, and He will lead us to repentance. Then we can get back to our walk with God.

18. **Romans 11:20** Well; **because of unbelief they were broken off**, and thou standest by faith. Be not highminded, but fear: 21 For if God spared not the natural branches, **take heed lest he also spare not thee.**

    - We need to fear living in sin. Having no fear equates to unbelief.

    - To fear God means to have a reverence and respect for His commands and understanding that there are consequences for not following those commands.

19. **Romans 11:22** Behold therefore the goodness and **severity of God**: on them which fell, **severity**; but toward thee, goodness, if thou continue in his goodness: **otherwise thou also shalt be cut off.** 23 And they also, if they abide not still in unbelief, shall be grafted in: for God is able to graft them in again.

Lesson 1 REPENTANCE

- Not looking at sin as severe and acting with indifference towards sin will lead to being cut off.

- If you believe as the Word says and repent, you can be grafted in again. This means going from lost, to being saved again.

20. **John 5:14** Afterward Jesus findeth him in the temple, and said unto him, Behold, thou art made whole: **sin no more**, lest a worse thing come unto thee.15 The man departed, and told the Jews that it was Jesus, which had made him whole.

- The man who was healed, and told to take up his bed and walk, was told by Jesus to sin no more, since he was now made whole.

- The warning from Jesus was, if he didn't repent, which is the definition of sinning no more, something worse than his previous condition could happen.

- Being made whole is a product of repentance. We are called to change our lives to live for Jesus according to his Word. If we don't stop sin, we can be sure that "worse" is around the corner. This also sounds like a good reason to repent to me.

21. **James 1:14** But every man is tempted, **when he is drawn away of his own lust, and enticed.** 15 Then when lust hath conceived, it bringeth forth sin: and sin, when it is finished, bringeth forth death.

- If we can learn where sin starts, then we can learn how to prevent it. Sin starts with temptation, and anyone can be tempted, even Jesus.

- However, we know that temptation is not a sin. We know this to be true because Jesus was tempted, but Jesus never sinned.

- The Word defines temptation as being drawn away by our own lust, and lust is where the enticement comes from.

- The Word tells us that unchecked lust turns into sin, and sin leads to death. This could be physical death, spiritual death, or both.

- It's not the first sin that usually gets us in trouble. It is the accumulation of sin that leads you away from God and makes you weak.

- Does that mean if you sin, destruction is an automatic fate? No. The sooner you repent, the weaker the hold sin has on you, and less damage is done. The longer you wait, the stronger the hold sin has on you, and the harder it will be to get out. If you wait too long, more damage is done, and you may never make it back.

22. **Hebrews 12:1** Wherefore seeing we also are compassed about with so great a cloud of witnesses, let us lay aside every weight, **and the sin which doth so easily beset us**, and let us run with patience the race that is set before us, **4 Ye have not yet resisted unto blood, striving against sin.**

- What Jesus wants from us, is to resist sin unto blood, and strive against it. This means to fight against sin with everything we have!

- Sin is very easy to fall into, however, when we strive to fight against it, we will be victorious.

- We tend to give up too easy. As a result, we end up breaking our covenant, or agreement with God. Fight harder!

23. **2 Peter 2:20** For if after they have escaped the pollutions of the world through the knowledge of the Lord and Saviour Jesus Christ, they are again entangled therein, and overcome, the latter end is worse with them than the beginning. **21 For it had been better for them not to have known the way of righteousness, than, after they have known it, to turn from the holy commandment delivered unto them.** 22 But it is happened unto them according to the true proverb, **the dog is turned to his own vomit again; and the sow that was washed to her wallowing in the mire.**

- Hell is already a sinner's fate. But, if someone gets saved and then goes back to sin, their fate is worse than their original fate. I think it's important to give a very real and direct description, of what the Lord is trying to show us.

- It's quite graphic and gross, but this is what God is trying to say. In verse 22, God equates sin to a dog eating his own throw-up and a pig rolling around in its own urine and feces. In this context, we are the dog and the pig.

- Ok, close your eyes and imagine yourself drinking a large glass of your own vomit… Then close your eyes and imagine yourself sitting in a tub of your own urine and feces… Do you feel sick right now? THIS IS HOW GOD FEELS ABOUT OUR SIN! This should cause us to see our sin the way God sees it, and not how we see it.

- People tend to minimize and justify sin. This will only lead to more sin. This image should help us reduce this negative practice.

24. **Matthew 7:21 Not everyone that saith unto me, Lord, Lord, shall enter into the kingdom of heaven;** but he that doeth the will of my Father which is in heaven. 22 Many will say to me in that day, Lord, Lord, **have we not prophesied in thy name?** and **in thy name have cast out devils?** and in thy name done many wonderful works? **23 And then will I profess unto them, I never knew you: depart from me, ye that work iniquity.**

- If the disgusting image of sin in 2 Peter doesn't motivate us to repent, maybe Matthew 7:23 will.

- These were people who preached the Word of God, were able to cast out devils, and did wonderful works of God, yet they were not able to go to heaven.

- Why? Even though they proclaimed to believe in Jesus, and had power in Jesus, their sin kept them from intimacy with Jesus. Jesus didn't know them because of their sin.

- God wants us to live sin-free, but if we mess up, His mercy gives us the opportunity to repent and keep moving forward with our walk with God. God does not give us an excuse to sin; He gives us a way out of sin. This is how God works with our humanity.

25. **John 8:34** Jesus answered them, Verily, verily, I say unto you, **whosoever committeth sin is the servant of sin.**

- We need to fight to keep ALL sin out of our lives. Even one sin, leads us to more. Sin never stays small, it always grows. When it's finished with you, then it will bring death (*James 1:15*).

26. **Romans 6:6** Knowing this, that our old man is crucified with him, that the body of **sin might be destroyed**, that henceforth we should not serve sin. 7 For he that is dead is freed from sin.

- When we repent, we are free from the bondage of sin. Liberty is the product of repentance.

27. **Romans 6:17** But God be thanked, that ye were the servants of sin, but ye have obeyed from the heart that form of doctrine which was delivered you. 18 **Being then made free from sin,** ye became the servants of righteousness.

- Again, as we saw in **1Corinthians 6:9**, The operative word "were", is past tense. As a servant of Jesus, we are not to stay in a constant state of sin. Sin is to be something of the past after conversion.

- When you become a doer of the Word and not a hearer only, is when you are made free from sin. **James 1:23** For if any be a hearer of the word, and not a doer, he is like unto a man beholding his natural face in a glass: **James 1:25** But whoso looketh into the perfect law of liberty, and continueth therein, **he being not a forgetful hearer, but a doer of the work, this man shall be blessed in his deed.**

- After the commitment to be a doer or to act in repentance, we can become a servant of righteousness. Then, we can begin our walk with God, and serve Him in whatever capacity he desires.

III. THE TRUE NATURE OF HOW SIN MAY OCCUR IN A CHRISTIAN'S LIFE

Based on what we know about the Word; this would be a normal progression of how a person may end up in sin:

- A person is born in sin.

- They get saved and start a relationship with God (**through Acts 2:38**).

- They begin to walk in the Spirit (**Galatians 5:16**).

- An external or internal conflict or crisis occurs that leads to enticement and temptation.

- The person begins to walk in the Spirit less and less (**Matthew 13:3-13**).

- As a result of persecution and/or temptation, the person sins.

- The person stays in sin and is Hell-bound or repents and is grafted in again with God.

CONCLUSION

- Everyone needs to REPENT!

- Everyone needs to fight daily to stay REPENTED!

- If you sin, don't give up, REPENT!

- You cannot go to Heaven without REPENTANCE!

- REPENTANCE is required for Salvation.

- REPENTANCE is the first step in God's salvation plan.

- God called Noah, Abraham, David, and Job perfect, but they all made mistakes.

- God's definition of perfection is not to never make a mistake, but how you respond to your mistakes. How a person responds to the sin they commit in their lives, determines the character of that person.

- However, you can REPENT perfectly every time sin takes place.

- How a Christian responds to their sin determines whether they are a hypocrite or not. People are sick of hypocritical behavior from church-going people who call themselves Christians. People are looking for the real deal.

Lesson 2
BAPTISM

In the Bible, baptism was approached with a sense of urgency. Baptism is often ignored or overlooked today. Most often when Baptism is taught, it is taught incorrectly. The purpose of Baptism is the remission of sins and the application of the blood of Jesus Christ to a person's life. Baptism is absolutely required for salvation. If a person doesn't submit to water baptism, do they really believe in Jesus?

1. **John 3:3** Jesus answered and said unto him, Verily, verily, I say unto thee, **Except a man be born again, he cannot see the kingdom of God**. 5 Jesus answered, Verily, verily, I say unto thee, **except a man be born of water and *of* the Spirit**, he cannot enter into the kingdom of God.

   - This passage is where the term "born-again Christian" comes from.

   - Born of water is submitting to water baptism by submersion and being born of the Spirit is receiving the baptism of Holy Ghost.

   - You MUST experience both or you cannot enter God's kingdom of Heaven. These words came directly from the mouth of Jesus.

   John 3:6 That which **is born of the flesh is flesh; and that which is born of the Spirit is spirit.**

   - Those who are advocates of the teaching that baptism is not required for salvation will teach that this verse determines that being born of water is referring to natural childbirth.

   - The first issue with that idea is that verse 3 says "born again," not initial birth. So being born of water is described as something happening after the natural childbirth.

   - The second issue with that mindset is it would mean that Jesus was commanding that a person be born naturally, or they couldn't see the kingdom of God. That doesn't make sense because everyone who is alive has been born.

   - The reason why this has even been challenged is that it doesn't fit the theology of those who teach against baptism as a part of a person's salvation.

- Lastly, and most importantly, that mindset completely contradicts the scriptures that are going to come next in this study. The Word will show clearly the purpose of baptism is the remission, or washing away of sin, and the application of the blood of Jesus.

2. **Mark 16:16** He that **believeth and is baptized** shall be **saved**; but he that believeth not shall be damned.

    - This demonstrates that more than belief is needed to be saved. The word "and" is an adjoining word that connects believing and baptism. If all a person had to do is believe without water baptism, the word "and" would not be there.

    - You MUST believe, which will lead to baptism. This is how they are connected.

    - If a person does not get baptized, they cannot receive remission of sins and their statement of belief should be questioned. There will be no sin in Heaven, so sin must be washed away before we can go there. Therefore, a person who claims to believe MUST be baptized.

3. **Acts 2:38** Then Peter said unto them, Repent, and be **baptized** every one of you in the name of Jesus Christ for the remission of sins, and ye shall receive the gift of the Holy Ghost.

    - This scripture gives us the who, how, and why of baptism. Who? Everyone. How? In the name of Jesus. Why? For the remission of sins. **The purpose of baptism is to wash away your sins in water by the blood of Jesus Christ.**

    - It is not the water that washes away sin, it is the blood of Jesus in the operation of baptism. So, this proves that baptism is where and when the blood of Jesus is applied to our lives.

4. **Revelation 1:5** And from Jesus Christ, who is the faithful witness, and the first begotten of the dead, and the prince of the kings of the earth. **Unto him that loved us, and washed us from our sins in his own blood,**

5. **1 John 1:7** But if we walk in the light, as he is in the light, we have fellowship one with another, **and the blood of Jesus Christ his Son cleanseth us from all sin.**

    - We know that sins are washed away in baptism, then according to these scriptures, it is a fact that the blood of Jesus is supernaturally applied to your life during water baptism.

- According to Peter and Jesus, baptism is to be done by submersion in water (*Acts 10:47, Mark 1:10 and Acts 8:39*).

- A person cannot go to heaven without the blood of Jesus, so the Lord gives us the mechanism to have His blood applied to us. This application takes place in water baptism.

6. **Acts 2:41** Then they that **gladly received his word** were baptized: and the same day there were added *unto them* about three thousand souls.

   - If someone does not get baptized, then they have not *gladly* received the Word like those on the day of Pentecost.

   - It was stated that the 3,000 were saved after they were baptized, not before. This also demonstrates that baptism is a part of salvation, the other parts being Repentance and receiving the Holy Ghost.

7. **Acts 22:16** And now why tarriest thou? arise, and be baptized, and **wash away thy sins**, calling on the name of the Lord.

   - The scripture tells us again that baptism washes away our sins.

   - If you have been taught that calling on the name of the Lord washes away the sin, then refer to all the previous scriptures mentioned in this lesson. That idea is not supported.

8. **Romans 6:4,6-7** Therefore we are buried with him by baptism into death: […] 6 Knowing this, that our old man is crucified with [him], that the **body of sin might be destroyed**, that henceforth we should not serve sin. 7 For he that is dead is freed from sin.

   - The Word is saying that the body of sin is destroyed in baptism, which supports the idea that the blood of Jesus Christ is applied to your life at that time. Only the blood of Jesus can wash away sin!

   - The usage of the word "buried", supports the idea of baptism by submersion. **Matthew 3:16** And Jesus, when he was baptized, went up straightway out of the water: and, lo, the heavens were opened unto him, and he saw the Spirit of God descending like a dove, and lighting upon him. **Jesus was submerged when he was baptized.** We should follow His example and be submerged.

9. **Acts 10:47** Can any man forbid water, that these should not be baptized, which have received the Holy Ghost as well as we? 48 **and he commanded them to be baptized** in the name of the Lord. Then prayed they him to tarry certain days.

- Peter recognized that the Gentiles had received the Holy Ghost and ordered them to be baptized immediately. They did so because Peter communicated a sense of urgency.

- The reason is, without baptism, a person has not had their sins washed away, and without remission of sin, there is no entry into Heaven.

- This passage confirms that people are to be baptized in water. If the passage said pickle juice, I would baptize in pickle juice. As a Pastor, I thank God it says water.

I. "BAPTISM IS ONLY SYMBOLIC, AND IS AN OUTWARD EXPRESSION OF AN INWARD FAITH"

- This statement is never made or even implied in the Word of God.

- The Word clearly tells us what God's purpose and intention are regarding baptism.

- In **1 Peter 3:20**, Noah, the ark, the water, and the people killed by the water were all symbolic. Baptism itself had a different, specific purpose. It wasn't just a symbol.

- That purpose is the mechanism of how our sins are washed away, and the blood of Jesus Christ is applied to our lives.

- Many churches teach that a person's baptism is just a symbol, or an outward expression of an inward faith. They don't believe that baptism washes away sins, and that baptism is a part of a person's salvation.

II. "BAPTISM DOES NOT WASH AWAY SIN"

- As you have already read, the Word of God says it does!

- Ironically, this is the position of most church organizations. Even the Baptist church. Baptist... Baptism?

III. "BAPTISM IS NOT A PART OF A PERSON'S SALVATION"

10. **1 Peter 3:20** Which sometime were disobedient, when once the longsuffering of God waited in the days of Noah, while the ark was a preparing, wherein few, that is, eight souls were saved by water. 21 The like figure whereunto even **baptism doth also now save us** (not the putting away of the filth of the flesh, but **the answer of a good conscience toward God**,) by the resurrection of Jesus Christ:

- Many churches do not believe that baptism washes away sins, and that baptism is a part of a person's salvation.

- Verse 20 tells us that Noah and the 8 souls were lifted by the ark above the sin and death. It says they were "saved by water."

- In Verse 21 it says that Noah and the ark are symbolic of baptism, but today baptism doth (or does) also NOW save us, meaning in the present. Noah and his family were saved by water before and we are saved by water now (in water baptism, along with Repentance and receiving the Holy Ghost).

- By using the word "also", implies that it is not ONLY baptism that saves you, but that baptism is a part of your salvation. **Acts 2:38** communicates the other parts of salvation.

- Why is it only a part of our salvation? Simply put, the two other components are also necessary for salvation.

- At that time, people would associate getting into a tub of water as taking a bath. So, it is made clear in the Word that it is not putting away the filth of the flesh or taking a physical bath, but it is getting sins washed away in a spiritual bath.

- The person who is baptized will have a good conscience toward God because they have done exactly what God has asked of them.

11. **Mark 16:16 He that believeth and is baptized shall be saved**; but he that believeth not shall be damned.

- Baptism is absolutely a part of our salvation!

- Here is another instance of the adjoining word "and" being used.

- By using the word "and" means that believing alone doesn't save a person, but believing and acting on that belief does.

Lesson 2 BAPTISM

- Without believing, a person will not get baptized, and they will be damned.

IV. DID THE THIEF ON THE CROSS NEED TO GET BAPTIZED IN ORDER TO BE SAVED?

- What about the thief on the cross? He was not baptized **Luke 23:43** "And Jesus said unto him, Verily I say unto thee, **to day shalt thou be with me in paradise,**"

- People often use the argument of the thief on the cross, that was positioned on the cross next to Jesus, as an example of why baptism is not required for salvation in the New Testament.

- Their thought is that the thief was not baptized, yet he was told that he would be in heaven with Jesus.

- The Bible clarifies this very directly.

12. **Hebrews 9:15** And for this cause **he [Jesus] is the mediator of the New Testament, that by means of death**, for the redemption of the transgressions *that were* under the first testament, they which are called might receive the promise of eternal inheritance. **16 For where a testament [is], there must also of necessity be the death of the testator.** 17 For a testament [is] of force after men are dead: otherwise it is of no strength at all while the testator liveth.

- This verse shows us that the New Testament does not start until after Jesus dies. The New Testament cannot start until Jesus gives up the ghost and sends it back for mankind to be filled.

- He does not give up the ghost until He dies on the cross. The Holy Ghost is sent to mankind in **Acts 2:4**, and that is when the New Testament starts, after the Salvation plan is preached in **Acts 2:38**.

- Obviously, when Jesus spoke to the thief on the cross, Jesus was alive. Therefore, the thief on the cross was saved under the old covenant law because the new covenant had not started yet.

- The fact is the thief on the cross did not have to be baptized. The thief would have been saved, but according to the Old Testament.

- When Jesus told the 10 lepers to go and show themselves to the priest as the Old Testament called for, demonstrates that the Old Testament was still in effect while Jesus was still alive. *Luke 5:14, and Luke 17:14 And when he saw them, he said unto them, **Go shew yourselves unto the priests**. And it came to pass, that, as they went, they were cleansed.*

V. TYPES AND SHADOWS OF BAPTISM IN THE OLD TESTAMENT

13. **1 Corinthians 10:1** Moreover, brethren, I would not that ye should be ignorant, how that all our fathers were under the cloud, and **all passed through the sea; 2 And were all baptized unto Moses** in the cloud and in the sea;

    - When the people of Israel crossed the Red Sea, they were considered to be baptized onto Moses.

    - The people didn't have to cross the Red Sea. They could have stayed on the shore of the sea without crossing. But what would have happened if they did stay onshore?

    - The answer is, they would have been killed by the Egyptians. So even though they didn't have to, they did if they didn't want to die.

    - This is an Old Testament type and shadow of the necessity of baptism in the New Testament. You don't have to get baptized, unless you want to live in eternity!

14. **Exodus 30:17** And the LORD spake unto Moses, saying, 18 Thou shalt also make a laver *of* brass, and his foot *also of* brass, **to wash** *withal*: and thou shalt put it between the tabernacle of the congregation and the altar, and thou shalt put water therein. **19 For Aaron and his sons shall wash their hands and their feet thereat:**

    - The Lord is the one telling Moses that the priests had to wash their hands and feet before entering the Holiest of Holies (*the inner chamber of the tabernacle*).

    Exodus 30:20 When they go into the tabernacle of the congregation, **they shall wash with water, that they die not**; or when they come near to the altar to minister, to burn offering made by fire unto the LORD: **21 So they shall wash their hands and their feet, that they die not**: and it shall be a statute for ever to them, *even* to him and to his seed throughout their generations.

    - If the priest did not wash at the laver before entering the Holiest of Holies, the priest would die.

- This is an Old Testament type and shadow of the necessity of baptism in the New Testament. No Baptism means No cleansing, which leads to no Salvation.

15. **1 Peter 3:20** Which sometime were disobedient, when once the longsuffering of God waited in the days of Noah, **while the ark was a preparing**, wherein few, that is, **eight souls were saved by water.** 21 **The like figure whereunto** *even* **baptism doth also now save us** (not the putting away of the filth of the flesh, but the answer of a good conscience toward God,) by the resurrection of Jesus Christ:

- The water lifted the boat and saved the 8 people and all the animals in the ark. This symbolizes that baptism is required for salvation today.

- The rebellious, sinful people in the water died in the flood. The water washed them away. The people who drowned were a symbol of sin, and the water is symbolic that baptism washes away sin.

- Noah and his family did not have to go on the boat as God told them, but if they didn't, they would have died with everyone else in the water. I would rather be on the boat!

- This is an Old Testament type and shadow of the necessity of baptism in the New Testament. No obedience leads to no cleansing, which leads to no Salvation.

CONCLUSION

- There will be no sin in Heaven. You can't go to Heaven until your sins have been washed away.

- The water does not wash your sins away; it is the blood of Jesus Christ.

- The blood of Jesus Christ is applied during Baptism.

- Water Baptism is required for God's Salvation!

- There is no scenario that one could present that would change this truth. If a man is dying on the side of the road and is not baptized before he dies, he does not have remission of sins. He does not have the blood; therefore, he cannot go to heaven. The best you can do is pray that he be healed, so he can do what God requires later.

- God is not unfair. There is no doubt that God would have attempted to reach that person numerous times, right up to the time his life was put in jeopardy. If he didn't listen, that is not God's fault. Just because he is scared and sincere at that moment, doesn't change God's requirements.

- Some people fear baptism because they fear they are going to mess up after they get baptized. Let me make it easy for you. You are going to mess up sometime after you get baptized. This is because NO ONE is perfect.

- If you sin after being baptized, you must repent and go back to living for God. You do not have to be re-baptized.

- When you are baptized, but sin and remain un-repented, you would be lost since you have sinned. If you die after backsliding, and you're not repented, you will be lost, and you will not be able to make Heaven your home.

- This is one of the greatest tragedies. A simple prayer of repentance from that person who was already baptized, but was backslidden, would have put them in heaven. This is true if they were refilled with the Holy Ghost after their repentance.

- You do not want to delay baptism for fear of messing up, just like you would not delay driving a new vehicle for fear of getting it dirty.

- If you have ever sinned, which you have, then get baptized and Jesus will wash away every sin you have ever committed.

- Get baptized for the remission of sins, study and learn all the scriptures about it, then teach others the beauty and necessity of baptism. You will be cleansed and blessed!

Lesson 3
THE HOLY GHOST

The Holy Ghost is simply the Spirit of God. The Holy Ghost gives us the power to be sin free. The Holy Ghost and the Holy Spirit are the same thing. The evidence that someone has received the initial filling of the Holy Ghost is when they begin to speak in tongues as the Spirit gives the utterance. Receiving the Holy Ghost is required to be saved. The evidence that someone is living under the power of the Holy Ghost is they will demonstrate, or operate in, the fruits of the Spirit. *Galatians 5:22 But the fruit of the Spirit **is love, joy, peace, longsuffering, gentleness, goodness, faith, 23 Meekness, temperance:** against such there is no law.*

1. **Acts 1:8** But **ye shall receive power**, after that the Holy Ghost is come upon you: and **ye shall be witness**es unto me both in Jerusalem, and in all Judaea, and in Samaria, and unto the uttermost part of the earth.

   - You cannot be a witness or a testimony if you do not have the power to stop your sin.

   - The Holy Ghost gives you that power to stop sin.

   - When we acquire the power to be free from sin, then we can be a witness or a testimony of God's power. (*Matthew 7:5-6*)

2. **Acts 2:4** And they were all filled with the Holy Ghost, and began to **speak with other tongues**, as the Spirit gave them utterance.

   - This passage refers to the 120 Jews that were in the upper room and filled with the Holy Ghost. Among them were the 12 disciples and Mary, the mother of Jesus. They all received the Holy Ghost.

   - After receiving the Holy Ghost, they came out of the upper room speaking in tongues and were full of mighty power. Speaking in tongues was evidence that they received the Holy Ghost.

   - Peter saw that this was a perfect time to preach to the people. Peter let them know what was happening and how they could be saved (*Acts 2:21*).

   - That is when he delivered God's salvation message in **Acts 2:38**.

3. **Acts 2:38** Then Peter said unto them, Repent, and be baptized every one of you in the name of Jesus Christ for the remission of sins, and ye shall receive the gift of **the Holy Ghost**.

   - Peter said receiving the Holy Ghost is what we will experience as a part of the salvation plan of God.

   - Some received the Holy Ghost first and then were baptized (*Acts 10:45-47*), and some were baptized first and then received the Holy Ghost (*Acts 19:5-6*). Either way is biblical.

4. **Acts 10:44** While Peter yet spake these words, the Holy Ghost fell on all them which heard the word. 45 And they of the circumcision which believed were astonished, as many as came with Peter, because that **on the Gentiles also was poured out the gift of the Holy Ghost. 46 For they heard them speak with tongues** and magnify God.

   - The Israelites (*Jews*) were with Peter and watched the Gentiles receive the Holy Ghost.

   - The Israelites were shocked because **they were the chosen people**. They were set aside from everyone else, to be the children of God at that time.

   - The Jews witnessed the Gentiles speak in tongues.

   - The word "for" demonstrates that speaking in tongues was the evidence that someone has received the Holy Ghost.

5. **Acts 19:2** He said unto them, **have ye received the Holy Ghost since ye believed?** And they said unto him, **we have not so much as heard whether there be any Holy Ghost.** 3 And he said unto them, Unto what then were ye baptized? And they said, Unto John's baptism. 4 Then said Paul, John verily baptized with the baptism of repentance, saying unto the people, that they should believe on him which should come after him, that is, on Christ Jesus. 5 When they heard this, they were baptized in the name of the Lord Jesus. 6 And when Paul had laid his hands upon them, the Holy Ghost came on them; and they spake with tongues, and prophesied.

   - When a person accepts the Lord as their personal Savior, do they automatically receive the Holy Ghost? This is a widely taught idea in modern-day Christianity today.

   - This passage proves, without a shadow of a doubt, that believing in Jesus does NOT automatically mean God fills a person with the Holy Ghost.

   - In Acts chapter 19 they believed, and were disciples, but did NOT have the Holy Ghost!

Lesson 3 THE HOLY GHOST

- Paul laid hands on them and they started to speak in tongues, which demonstrates that they received the Holy Ghost. Then they were water baptized (*fulfillment of Acts 2:38*).

6. **Mark 16:17** And these signs shall follow them that believe; In my name shall they cast out devils; **they shall speak with new tongues**.

    - Jesus said it clearly, a believer will speak in tongues.

    - The same Greek word "glossa" (Strongs' 1100 gloce-sah), is used in both Acts 10:46 and **Mark 16:17** for the word tongues.

    - Therefore, the speaking in tongues in **Acts 10:46**, that related to receiving the Holy Ghost, is the same speaking in new tongues of **Mark 16:17**, which follow them that believe.

    - This supports the fact that when someone receives the initial infilling of the Holy Ghost, as a result of their belief, they will speak in tongues.

    - After that initial infilling, a Spirit-filled person will speak in tongues as they edify or build themselves up spiritually. This usually takes place during worship or prayer, but it can also happen while simply meditating on the Lord.

7. **Romans 8:8-9** So then they that are in the flesh cannot please God. 9 But ye are not in the flesh, but in the Spirit, if so be that the Spirit of God dwell in you. **Now if any man have not the Spirit of Christ, he is none of his.**

    - If someone does not have the Holy Ghost, they are not His (*they do not belong to Jesus Christ*). If you are not His, you cannot go to Heaven.

    - This is also true of Repentance and Baptism.

    - You need all three to fulfill the Salvation Plan of Jesus!

8. **John 16:12** I have yet many things to say unto you, but ye cannot bear them now. 13 Howbeit when he, the Spirit of truth, is come, **he will guide you into all truth:** for he shall not speak of himself; but whatsoever he shall hear, that shall he speak: and he will shew you things to come.

    - We are to receive the Holy Ghost and be led to the Truth.

    - If you do not have the Holy Ghost, can you be led to the Truth? Nope.

- An Apostolic should be careful not to debate doctrinal Truth with anyone who is NOT filled with the Holy Ghost!

- If someone does not have the Holy Ghost, how can they be guided into all Truth? But, if a person is eager to learn about Jesus and salvation, they should be taught this study. Just do not debate any topics until they have received the Holy Ghost.

I. SPEAKING WITH TONGUES

- First, let's clarify that Jesus never **spoke in tongues**. He was God in the flesh and had no need to be edified, or built up, as we do. Therefore, there is no record of Jesus **speaking in tongues**.

- Jesus was taken up into the clouds *Acts 1:9 And when he had spoken these things, while they beheld, **he was taken up; and a cloud received him out of their sight**.* Then, Jesus gave up the ghost (*the Spirit*), and sent back the Holy Ghost, so mankind would be filled with his Spirit, as a part of the Salvation plan of God.

- Jesus was not on this earth when **speaking in tongues** began in the book of Acts. That is another reason why there is no record of Jesus **speaking in tongues**.

- **Speaking with tongues,** or divers **tongues** simply means supernaturally speaking in another language other than your native tongue, which could be human or angelic. *1 Corinthians 13:1 Though I speak with the **tongues of men and of angels**...*

- **Speaking with tongues** usually happens when a person, or group of people, are praising and worshipping in the Spirit. Then the children of God begin to **speak with tongues**. They are built up spiritually because they are submitting to God in prayer and worship.

- During one's initial infilling of the Holy Ghost, **speaking with tongues** takes place. **Speaking in tongues** continues to occur during times of prayer, praise, and worship. **Speaking in tongues** is to edify or build up a believer. (*1 Corinthians 14:4*)

- **Speaking with tongues** is a sign to them that don't believe. They see this supernatural power, and it becomes a sign of God's power to the unbeliever. *1 Corinthians 14:22* **Wherefore tongues are for a sign,** *not to them that believe,* **but to them that believe not:** *but prophesying serveth not for them that believe not, but for them which believe.*

Lesson 3 THE HOLY GHOST

- When someone sees the power of God working in people who are **speaking in tongues**, it is supposed to help them believe as it did with Simon the Sorcerer in **Acts 8**. It appears that is what he saw that made him want to give money to acquire the same power. Details on that event and how it happened will come later in the lesson.

II. NEW TONGUES, OTHER TONGUES, UNKNOWN TONGUES, AND TONGUES AND INTERPRETATION

There are 4 types of **speaking in tongues** that we will discuss. Speaking in a **New Tongue**, **Other Tongues**, **Unknown Tongues** and **Tongues and Interpretation.** These are all spiritual gifts.

A. New Tongues

- **New tongues** are mentioned in the book of Mark. *Mark 16:17 And these signs shall follow them that believe; In my name shall they cast out devils; **they shall speak with new tongues**.*

- **New tongues** are supernaturally speaking in a different language than your native tongue as a product of belief. This is a **spiritual gift** that happens when someone receives the **gift of the Holy Ghost**.

B. Other Tongues

- **Other tongues** are also supernaturally speaking in a different language than your native tongue. It is a **spiritual gift** that happens when someone receives the **gift of the Holy Ghost**.

- The speaker does not know the language he or she is speaking, but the hearer does, if the **other tongue** was in their language. In short, a **tongue** other than one's own.

- The biblical example of **other tongues** is found in **Acts** chapter **2:4-6.** Those that followed Jesus, went to the upper room by his command.

- The Holy Ghost fell, and they came out of that room **speaking with tongues. Acts 2:4** And they were all filled with the Holy Ghost, and **began to speak with other tongues**, as the **Spirit gave them utterance.** 6 Now when this was noised abroad, the multitude came together, and were confounded, because that **every man heard them speak in his own language.** This **other tongue** was the evidence that they had received the Holy Ghost (*like in Acts 10:44-45*).

- The **other tongues** in Acts 2 were a language not known to the Jews as they spoke it, but those that heard it, knew it was their language. There were 16 languages spoken on that day (*the day of Pentecost*).

C. Unknown Tongues

- The **unknown tongue** is supernaturally speaking in a language that no man or woman knows. *1 Corinthians 14:2 For he that speaketh in an unknown tongue speaketh not unto men, but unto God: for no man understandeth him; howbeit in the spirit he speaketh mysteries.*

- Angelic languages would be an **unknown tongue**, as no one can say they understand angelic languages. The apostle Paul said that he spoke in angelic and foreign languages when he **spoke with tongues.** *1 Corinthians 13:1 Though I speak with the tongues of men and of angels....*

- The Word of God says a person who is speaking in an **unknown tongue** should pray for the **unknown tongue** to be interpreted. If God answers that prayer, that person, or someone else, will give the translation of what God said in the **unknown tongue** (*1Corinthians 14:13*).

- The **unknown tongue** that is translated is still unknown to the speaker. **The unknown tongue** supernaturally becomes known to the person who is called by the Spirit to receive it. Then that person gives the interpretation to the church. The church will hear it and be blessed.

- This is when the unknown tongue stops being the unknown tongue and becomes **tongues and interpretation.**

D. Tongues and Interpretation

- **Tongues and interpretation** take place in some type of Church assembly, but not everyone has or operates in, this gift.

- When people do have this gift, some may operate in the **tongues** portion, some may operate the **interpretation** portion, and some may operate in both. Many will not operate in either part of that gift. **Especially if it's not believed in or sought after.**

- This gift generally involves individuals who have a higher level of intimacy and maturity in the Spirit, **that is why not everyone has this gift.** However, it is possible for newer folks to be used in this gift as well.

- **Tongues and interpretation** cannot happen when someone is by themselves. Both an interpreter, and people to be edified by what is being interpreted, are needed (*1Corinthians 14:5*).

- **Tongues and interpretation** have two parts. Someone **speaks in tongues** and the same person, or another person gives the interpretation.

- **Tongues and interpretation** happen during the times when born-again believers are gathered, are deeply connected to who and what Jesus really is and connected to his purpose.

- The level of intimacy with Jesus is increased, and the likelihood that the gifts of the Spirit will take place, also increases.

- Not everyone has this gift, but it appears that anyone who seeks it, could operate in it over time, with increased spiritual maturity.

- Those who are being called to be used in this gift also must submit to it. God will not force it on people. This is a powerful experience, and often quite scary, therefore, submission is necessary.

III. DOES EVERY BELIEVER SPEAK WITH TONGUES?

- One of the biggest misinterpretations about **tongues,** is the teaching that not every Christian will **speak in tongues**.

- The rationale given to why some feel that not everyone will speak with **Tongues** is because **Tongues** is a gift and not everyone has it.

- The truth is, every Christian **will not be involved specifically in the gift of tongues and interpretation**. However, **speaking with tongues** is a gift that is an essential part of a Christian's life.

- The gift of tongues is the evidence that you have received the gift of the Holy Ghost. Everyone must receive the Holy Ghost to be a believer. **Therefore, every believer will speak in tongues** (*Mark 16:17*). This makes perfect biblical sense.

- The Word is going to determine that there is a difference between the **speaking with tongues/unknown tongue** and **tongues and interpretation**. This is determined by the purpose of each and who is edified by it.

- Understanding that difference, will answer the question of whether every believer will **speak with tongues** or not.

- The simple answer is yes, all believers will **speak with tongues**. We will spend a considerable amount of time giving the scripture and commentary that will reveal this to be true.

- There are a lot of important details to cover in **1Corinthians** chapter **14** that answers this question.

9. **1 Corinthians 14:1** Follow after charity, and desire spiritual gifts, but rather that ye may prophesy. **1 Corinthians 14:2** For he that speaketh in an **unknown tongue speaketh not unto men, but unto God: for no man understandeth him;** howbeit in the spirit he speaketh mysteries.

- Believers need to desire for and seek out spiritual gifts. Prophecy is when a person speaks under divine inspiration (*preaching, teaching, foretelling, or a prediction that must come true*).

- Speaking in an **unknown tongue** was not "unto man," and no man could understand it, **so there would be no interpretation** of that **tongue. Tongues and interpretation** deliver a message for the church.

- Therefore, **unknown tongues** and **tongues and interpretation** would have to be different. They are also different in their purpose. Verses 4 and 5 will show us how.

4 He that **speaketh in an unknown tongue edifieth himself**; but he that prophesieth edifieth the church.

- **Speaking with tongues/unknown tongues** edifies, or builds up, a person spiritually.

5 I would that ye all spake with tongues, but rather that ye prophesied: for greater is he that prophesieth **than he that speaketh with tongues, except he interpret**, that the **church may receive edifying**.

- Paul states that everybody has the ability to **speak with tongues**. It is not limited to certain people. Paul desired to see all people **speak with tongues**.

- Prophesy is a divinely inspired foretelling of future events, or the super-natural, sudden impulse to edify the body of Christ. Prophesy is greater than speaking in an **unknown tongue**.

- That is because Prophecy is not just an individual being edified by God as in **speaking with tongues**. But the whole church will be edified, from the prophecy given from the Word of God or the Spirit of God.

- Prophecy is preferred over **speaking with tongues** unless there is an **interpretation of tongues**. But when there are **tongues and interpretation** it is preferred over Prophesy.

- When **unknown tongues/speaking with tongues** are interpreted, it is preferred over Prophecy because not only does it also edifies the church, but because the explanation of the **unknown tongues comes directly from God and not the servant of God**.

- These passages prove that **unknown tongues** and **tongues and interpretation** are both spiritual gifts. Notice, the Word uses **unknown tongues** (*verse 2*) and **speaking with tongues** (*verse 5*), synonymously. This is because they are the same.

- It would make sense that if a person sought after Spiritual gifts and seeks to walk in the Spirit with all their heart, that person would acquire those spiritual gifts.

IV. THE MEANING OF "DO ALL SPEAK WITH TONGUES? DO ALL INTERPRET?"

- The passage used most often to present the ideas that not all Christians will **speak in tongues** is from **1 Corinthians 12:30** *Have all the gifts of healing? **do all speak with tongues? do all interpret?***

- Going back to *1 Corinthians 12:10 To another the working of miracles; to another prophecy; to another discerning of spirits; to another **divers kinds of tongues; to another the interpretation of tongues**,* shows that verse 30 is referring to the gift of **tongues and interpretation**.

- Verse 10 mentions **tongues and interpretation** and verse 30 questions whether everyone does it. Therefore, what that verse is saying is, not everyone will operate in the gift of **tongues and interpretation. It is not referring to regular speaking in tongues.**

- However, we have clearly proven that **tongues and interpretation** is a different gift than speaking with **tongues/unknown tongues**.

- This fact is essential to understanding why it is incorrect to teach that not everyone will **speak with tongues**. All believers will **speak with tongues**.

- **Mark 16:17** states that **all believers will Speak in Tongues**, and **1 Corinthian 12:9-10,29-30**, states that **not all believers will give Tongues and Interpretation**.

- **Those that believe in Jesus** will speak in New Tongues, *Mark 16:17 And these signs shall follow them that believe; In my name shall they cast out devils; **they shall speak with new tongues.***

- The believer has their original tongue or language, but when they receive the Holy Ghost, they will **speak in tongues**. So, it is false teaching to say that all Christians do not speak in tongues.

- When the New Testament Church first begins in the book of Acts, people did not have to reach a certain level of spiritual maturity and spiritual growth to speak in **tongues**. The Bible shows that speaking in **tongues** happened when people received the Holy Ghost.

- In short, speaking in an **unknown tongue/speaking with tongues** is a Spiritual gift that will happen to all that are filled with the Holy Ghost, either for the first time or when they seek to be built up in the faith. **Tongues and interpretation** is a Spiritual gift as well, **but not everyone has, or is used in that gift**.

- It has been my personal experience that when the church is worshipping deeply, the Spirit will take the church to another level of intimacy. The Spirit moves in a tremendously powerful way, and these gifts begin to manifest in the church.

- It is more beneficial and productive spiritually if we understand how this process works. That is the purpose of spending so much time on it and why there is so much repetition.

V. CAN A PERSON RECEIVE THE HOLY GHOST WITHOUT SPEAKING IN TONGUES?

- Many believe that someone can receive the Holy Ghost, even if they have not spoken in **tongues**. However, **Acts 10:45-46** makes it clear that **speaking in tongues** was the evidence that **the Gentiles** received the Holy Ghost.

- In **Acts 2:4-5** we can see that **the Jews** spoke in **other tongues** when they received the Holy Ghost. The fact is, every time someone received the Holy Ghost in the book of Acts, except one, they **spoke in tongues**.

- In that one instance, Simon the Sorcerer saw something happen when people received the Holy Ghost that was so amazing, that he wanted to pay the apostles for the power to duplicate it (*Act 8:18-19*).

- It appears, that this was referring to **speaking in tongues**, as he had already seen healing, miracles, and wonders. Since people spoke with tongues, all the other time the Holy Ghost was given, it is not a stretch to believe that Simon the Sorcerer saw them **speak with tongues.**

- Many **people today are open to receiving the Holy Ghost**. It just isn't taught enough or appropriately. The simple solution is to teach people about the Spirit and lead them to receive the gift of the Holy Ghost, evidenced by the gift of tongues. **This kind of emphasis will increase the likelihood of people receiving ghost in the churc**h.

- If someone is in a church that is teaching that sin is a natural part of a Christian's life, then this teaching is what is keeping them from receiving the Holy Ghost according to **Romans 8:4-8** *"That the righteousness of the law might be fulfilled in us, **who walk not after the flesh, but after the Spirit. 5 For they that are after the flesh do mind the things of the flesh; but they that are after the Spirit the things of the Spirit. 6 For to be carnally minded is death;** but to be spiritually minded is life and peace. 7 **Because the carnal mind is enmity against God: for it is not subject to the law of God, neither indeed can be. 8 So then they that are in the flesh cannot please God**."*

- A person who is in the flesh is not Repented as the scripture says. Therefore, they cannot receive the Holy Ghost, which in turn means, they will not speak in tongues.

- Lead people to repentance and have them seek the Holy Ghost, evidence by **speaking in tongues**, and watch God work.

VI. IS IT A BAD THING TO SEEK TO EDIFY YOURSELF SPIRITUALLY?

- When people in the modern-day Christian church are shown the concepts of how edification is connected to speaking in tongues, they often respond by saying that the word "edifieth", in the context of **1Corinthians 14:4**, has a negative meaning. They believe it means to lift oneself up, to be prideful, to be puffed up, or to be boastful.

- "Edifieth", comes from the Greek word, **Oikodomeo**, and according to the Strong's concordance, it simply means allowing yourself to be built up by God's Spirit. **It is in no way negative, to build yourself up spiritually. As a matter of fact, it is a spiritual necessity.**

- In the second part of verse 4, it says the church is edified by prophecy. The same Greek word, **Oikodomeo**, is used for "edifieth" in both parts of verse 4. *1Corinthians 14:4 He that speaketh in an [unknown] tongue **edifieth himself**; but he that prophesieth **edifieth the church**.*

- Clearly, the word of God is not saying that prophecy makes the church puffed up or prideful, in the second part of verse 4. This means it has the same positive meaning in the first and second part of verse 4.

VII. IF THERE IS NO INTERPRETATION OF AN UNKNOWN TONGUE, AM I SUPPOSED TO STOP SPEAKING IN TONGUES?

- I have had many people, from modern-day Christianity, tell me that if there is speaking in **unknown tongues**, and no one to interpret, then the person is to stop speaking in tongues. They get this idea from **1 Corinthians 14:28** But if there be **no interpreter, let him keep silence** in the church; **and let him speak to himself, and to God.**

- This passage is specifically referring to the tongues portion of **tongues and interpretation**. It is not talking about the **unknown tongues or speaking in tongues** mentioned earlier in this chapter. If it was, it would mean the only time people can **speak in tongues** is if interpretation follows it. **This is a limitation God does not impose.**

- How can we be so sure that it is referring to the **tongues** portion of **tongues and interpretation**? *1 Corinthians 14:27 If any man speak in an [unknown] tongue, [let it be] by two, or at the most [by] three, and [that] by course; and **let one interpret**.* **This passage is not** just talking **about speaking in tongues** by itself.

- Verse 27 also introduces the idea that this reference is about **tongues and interpretation** because it says, **"let one interpret"**. This idea is also confirmed again in verse 28 by saying **"if there be no interpreter"**, which means the context is in relation to **tongues and interpretation** and **not just speaking in tongues**.

- When a person comprehends the concept of **unknown tongues** and **tongues and interpretation** as established earlier, the answer to this one is easy. There is no interpretation when the **tongue is unknown**. It is not unto man, but unto God, no man understands it. *1Corinthians 14:2 "For he that speaketh in an unknown tongue speaketh **not unto men**, but unto God: for **no man understandeth him**; howbeit in the spirit he speaketh mysteries."*

Lesson 3 THE HOLY GHOST

- There can be **no interpretation** of something that is **not supposed to be interpreted**. Therefore, when it says **"keep silent"**, the word is referring to the times when God is attempting to operate in the gifts of **tongues and interpretation**, and the person who is **speaking in tongues** does not submit to receiving the interpretation, and no one in the gathering received the interpretation to give to those in attendance. At that point they are to **be silent and speak to themselves and God.**

- Therefore, being silent does not refer to the church not speaking in tongues anymore. It's referring to the call to abandon and further seeking of **tongues and interpretation**.

- God may also try to give someone else in the room the interpretation. If that person does not submit to receiving and speaking the interpretation, they are also supposed to **be silent and speak to themselves and God.**

- At this point the operation shifts. It goes from being **tongues and interpretation** back to **the unknown tongue** that edifies the individual and not the church. This is only because there was **no interpretation**. If there is **no interpretation the person is to stop seeking interpretation, but not necessarily stop speaking in tongues**.

- We can say this because in *1 Corinthians 14:2 For he that speaketh in an unknown tongue speaketh not unto men, **but unto God,*** is saying that speaking in an **unknown tongue** is also considered **speaking unto God**. This gives us even more evidence that when there is **no interpretation it does not mean you are supposed to stop speaking in tongues.**

- In verse 27, there is an added detail to have the church only operate in the course of threes when **tongues and interpretation** happens. This is solely to keep order because the Corinthian church was often out of order. Course of three could be tongue and interpretation three times, or tongues three times and three interpretations, or any combination of the tongue and interpretation, but only three times.

- It is easy to see how people could make the mistake of thinking tongues was only allowed with an interpretation. However, **rightly dividing the word of truth makes it easy** to correct this mistake and bring clarity to whomever is asking.

- We can now see the error in saying that a person must stop **speaking in tongues** if there is not an interpretation of an **unknown tongue**. When the shift is made away from **tongues and interpretation**, to being only an **unknown tongue,** is not intended to be interpreted any longer. **It would be for self-edification purposes only.**

- It is now clear, if **tongues and interpretation** does not happen, the church may continue speaking in an **unknown tongue** as the service continues, as the church members edify themselves in the Lord. Speaking in tongues is one of the essential components of the church and edification should not be hindered. **To do so would be considered quenching the Spirit,** *1Thesselonions 5:19 Quench not the Spirit.*

- This may explain why many churches are not very lively or on fire for God. Unfortunately, most churches quench the Spirit of God. As a result, the plans the Lord has for revival in the church are also hindered.

VIII. SPEAKING IN TONGUES IS OF THE DEVIL?

10. 1 Corinthians 14:18 I thank my God, I speak with tongues more than ye all. 22 Wherefore **tongues are for a sign**, not to them that believe, **but to them that believe not**: but prophesying serveth not for them that believe not, but for them which believe. 39 Wherefore, brethren, covet to prophesy, and **forbid not to speak with tongues**. 40 Let all things be done decently and in order.

- If speaking in tongues was of the devil, these scriptures would not be in the Bible. The apostle Paul spoke in tongues, so **nobody should ever be forbidden to speak in tongues.**

- Speaking in tongues took place consistently in the New Testament, and it is even classified as being decent and in order (*1Corithinians 14:40*). If you never speak in tongues, are you in order?

- Speaking in tongues is to edify (*build up*) a person in prayer and worship, and it is a sign to the unbeliever. **The only one who would want to restrict tongues, would be the devil.**

- The devil will mimic things of God and may mimic tongues. These tongues are not of God but are of the devil. There is always evidence in that person, that they are not of God.

- It will always come out sooner or later. **Numbers 32:23** "But if ye will not do so, behold, ye have sinned against the LORD: and **be sure your sin will find you out.**"

- These **demonic manifestations** (*demonic possession*), rarely happen in a church full of the Holy Ghost. The enemy hates the powerful presence of God and in my nearly 20 years in the church, I have never seen it.

Lesson 3 THE HOLY GHOST

- The worst thing I have seen is people gaging when they seek the Holy Ghost. They usually have an evil spirit that is easily cast out by the power of God's Spirit.

- **If anyone, or any church, forbids people to speak in tongues, they are not acting scriptural, according to the apostle Paul.**

IX. WHY SPEAKING IN TONGUES?

11. James 3:3 Behold, we put **bits in the horses' mouths**, that they may obey us; and we **turn about their whole body. 8 But the tongue can no man tame**; *it is* an unruly evil, full of deadly poison.

- If the Lord can control us from our mouth/tongue, he can guide our whole body.

- No man can tame the tongue, except God. That is why it appears that God decided to **use speaking in tongues to demonstrate that the Holy Ghost is abiding in a person's body**.

- Human beings build relationships with each other by speaking verbally. **When we speak in tongues**, a **relationship is being developed** between us and God.

- This is another reason why, it appears, that the Lord uses the mouth/tongue, to speak a heavenly language, **to determine that someone has received the Holy Ghost.**

12. 1 Corinthians 13:1 Though I speak with the tongues of men and of angels, and have not charity, I am become [as] sounding brass, or a tinkling cymbal.

- The sounds and syllables that come out of a person when they are speaking in tongues vary tremendously.

- Sometimes, it may sound crazy, quiet, loud, our even may sound like gibberish.

- No one should judge their tongues, or another person's tongues, unless you know all the known, and unknown human, and angelic languages. Of course, no person does.

- There may be known languages being spoken, but linguists would not know any angelic languages. This verse determines that it is a useless task to bring linguists to a Pentecostal church to determine the legitimacy of speaking in tongues.

- These are uncomfortable truths for many who have not spoken in **tongues**. People fight the idea of **speaking in tongues** being for everyone because it doesn't match their theology. **Not because it is not in the Bible**.

- People need to decide whether it is more important to **follow what they have been taught** in the past, **or what the Bible specifically says**.

X. SPEAKING IN TONGUES WILL CEASE?

13. **1 Corinthians 13:8** Charity never faileth: but whether *there be* prophecies, they shall fail; whether *there be* **tongues, they shall cease;** whether *there be* **knowledge, it shall vanish away.** 9 For we know in part, and we prophesy in part. 10 But **when that which is perfect is come, then that which is in part shall be done away.**

- There are those who use this scripture, to state that speaking in tongues is not for today. They proclaim, "that which is perfect is come", refers to Jesus coming.

- They think when Jesus came to present the gospel to mankind, speaking in tongues ceased. Not only is that not true, but the opposite is true. When Jesus came, preached, died, and was resurrected, is when tongues started.

- The problem with that mindset is that the Corinthian church was established on the **Acts 2:38** salvation, which included **receiving the Holy Ghost, evidence by speaking in other tongues. This would be after Jesus came and preached, died, and was resurrected.**

- What it appears the passage is really referring to is when Jesus comes back to claim his church in the rapture. **That is when tongues will cease because we will not need tongues in the 1000-year reign of Christ on Earth, or in the eternity** we will spend in heaven.

- There will be **no need to be edified** any longer because **we will have a glorified body**, so tongues will not be necessary.

- There is another problem with the mindset that tongues are not for today's time. If the understanding is that **tongues are going to cease**, then that means **knowledge is going to have to cease at the same time**. That is obviously not true.

- If it is **not true that knowledge will cease**, then it's also **not true that tongues will cease**.

- **1Corinthians 13:8 cannot** be saying that tongues will stop. **Why?** Because Paul the apostle specifically spoke about tongues and tongues and interpretation in the very next chapter of **1Corinthians 14**. As a matter of fact, the whole chapter is on speaking in tongues, and Paul said forbid not to speak in tongues.

- Any teaching that speaking in tongues is not for today's time is **false doctrine**. That teaching usually **comes from those who do not have the Holy Ghost**, evidence by speaking in tongues. **Those individuals are usually looking to provide a reason why they do not speak in tongues.**

- Tongues as evidence of receiving the Holy Ghost does not fit their theology. **But it fits the theology of Jesus.**

- If a person is not taught this biblical principle of speaking in tongues, but is taught that a person will not necessarily speak in tongues when the Holy Ghost fills a person, then **speaking in tongues is less likely to happen**. This is not consistent with the teaching of the apostle Paul, and it is not of God.

- If a person seeks the Holy Ghost, the Lord will fill them, that is His promise. When they are filled, they will speak in tongues.

CONCLUSION

- The Holy Ghost is the source of Apostolic Christian's power.

- Without the Holy Ghost we cannot go to Heaven.

- Receiving the baptism of the Holy Ghost is a part of the plan of Salvation.

- We know that the initial sign of receiving the Holy Ghost is when we speak in tongues, as the Spirit gives the utterance. This will happen to ALL believers when they receive the Holy Ghost.

- Every believer will experience speaking in tongues, and he or she is built up spiritually when it happens. There is no minimum or maximum of how often people will speak in tongues. That may vary from person to person.

- Not every believer gives the tongues portion of tongues and interpretation, and not every believer gives the interpretation portion of **tongues and interpretation**. **Tongues and interpretation** is a spiritual gift, but not everyone has it.

- If the concepts of speaking in tongues are not understood, many people won't get the Holy Ghost as a result.

- If the spiritual gifts of tongues and interpretation are sought after by an individual, they will most likely operate in those gifts at some point in their walk with God.

Lesson 4
WALKING IN THE SPIRIT

Walking in the Spirit, leads to, **living** in the Spirit. It is also an essential component of successfully **maintaining a repented life**. If walking in the Spirit is going to prevent us from sinning, it is essential to find out how to do it and do it right. Therefore, the Lord led me to write this lesson in the Kingdom Bible Study. I have never seen a Bible study on this specific subject, yet it might be one of the most important Bible studies to teach today.

I studied the specific behaviors the Lord desires of us, which would lead to an increase in spiritual strength. The following scriptures are just some of the passages that describe those behaviors and how they apply to one's spiritual strength. It takes an increased level of discipline to be successful in walking in the Spirit. We must choose to walk in the Spirit, otherwise, we are choosing to sin. There is a consequence for choosing to sin, and those consequences can, and should, be avoided.

1. **Galatians 5:16** This I say then, **Walk in the Spirit**, and ye **shall not fulfil the lust of the flesh.**

   Galatians 5:25 If we live in the Spirit, let us also walk in the Spirit.

   - This may be one of the most important passages in the Bible.

   - The obvious question should be: How do we walk in the Spirit?

   - The answer to this question will show us how to live free from sin. Living free of sin is referred to 16 times in Romans chapter 6. This is God's will for us!

   - When we live each day choosing not to sin, we will have learned how to fulfill **2 Corinthians 7:9-10**, which is to repent and stay repented.

   - Below are 10 major approaches to reach the goal of walking in the Spirit.

I. 10 WAYS TO WALK IN THE SPIRIT

1. *FAITHFULNESS* – **Hebrews 10:25 Not forsaking the assembling of ourselves together**, as the manner of some is; but exhorting one another: **and so much the more, as ye see the day approaching.**

   - We need to come together as a church for fellowship and spiritual support. We need to be at church whenever the doors are open.

   - The church is where a person gets their regular spiritual feeding. Less Church leads to going hungry spiritually. This makes a person weaker and more vulnerable.

   - We need to be in church more, especially in these last days.

   - Will going to church regularly, and participating in the service make us spiritually stronger? YES!

2. *BIBLE READING* - **2 Timothy 2:15 Study to shew thyself approved unto God, a** workman that needeth not to be ashamed, **rightly dividing the word of truth.**

   - We **MUST** study the Bible, and **follow it**, so God will approve of our actions.

   - It takes work, but it's work we can be proud of. It's work we must do and **do diligently**. Life will always get busy. However, we must get back on track if a busy life slows, or stops, our Bible reading.

   - Will reading our Bibles make us spiritually stronger? YES!

3. *PRAYER* - **Matthew 26:41 Watch and pray, that ye enter not into temptation:** the spirit indeed [is] willing, **but the flesh [is] weak.**

   - Prayer is a way to communicate and receive direction from God.

   - We must be careful of what we do when living for God.

   - More temptation will come without prayer.

   - Even if we are sincere about prayer in our spirit, our flesh can cause us to fail, if we do not pray consistently.

Lesson 4 WALKING IN THE SPIRIT

- Life will always get busy, but we must get back on track with praying if a busy life slows, or stops, our praying/prayer life.

- Will praying make us spiritually stronger? YES!

4. *GROUP BIBLE STUDIES* – **2 Timothy 3:16** All scripture is given by inspiration of God, and is **profitable for doctrine, for reproof, for correction, for instruction in righteousness:**

- The Word is from God. It is the instructions we **NEED** to live by.

- The Word will instruct us on how to live in **His** righteousness.

- Everyone should be either **receiving** or **teaching** Bible studies, or **both.**

- If there is an error in our walk with God, the Word **WILL** reveal it.

- We should be **committed** to letting the Word lead us into **whatever corrections** necessary. Then we can demonstrate our obedience to God.

- Will teaching and studying the Bible make us spiritually stronger? YES!

5. *MENTORSHIP/DISCIPLESHIP* - **Matthew 28:18** And Jesus came and said to them, "All authority in heaven and on earth has been given to me. 19 **Go therefore and make disciples** of all nations….

- Discipleship is one of the hardest jobs of being a Christian.

- It is also one of the most rewarding and important.

- To disciple a person, you must learn how to be a mentor.

- **Galatians 6:1** Brethren, if a man be overtaken in a fault, ye which are spiritual, **restore such an one in the spirit of meekness**; considering thyself, lest thou also be tempted. 2 Bear ye one another's burdens, and so fulfil the law of Christ.

- Discipleship is how we protect and rely on each other. A mentor is designed to restore the fallen with compassion and mercy, without being judgmental. Discipleship also strengthens and protects the mentor as he or she serves the mentee.

- If you do not learn to disciple people, you may not stay saved. **Matt 25:30** "And cast ye the unprofitable servant into outer darkness: there shall be weeping and gnashing of teeth." Therefore, witnessing and/or discipleship is a salvation issue. This verse is about increase of the Kingdom, to include reaching the lost.

- **2 Timothy 2:1** Thou therefore, my son, be strong in the grace that is in Christ Jesus. 2 and the things that thou hast heard of me among many witnesses, **the same commit thou to faithful men, who shall be able to teach others also.** 3 Thou therefore endure hardness, as a good soldier of Jesus Christ.

- It is important to make sure that you are strong in grace.

- Those faithful men shall teach others about the grace of God, and as a result, the greatness of God will be spread in your community.

- It is hard work. So, endure it, if you want to be a good soldier of Jesus.

- Will becoming a mentor as a believer, or having a mentor as a new convert make us spiritually stronger? YES!

6. ***OBEDIENCE*** - **Deuteronomy 11:1** Therefore thou shalt love the LORD thy God, and **keep his charge, and his statutes, and his judgments, and his commandments, always.**

    - **2 Corinthians 10:5** Casting down imaginations, and every high thing that exalteth itself against the knowledge of God, and **bringing into captivity every thought to the obedience of Christ;**

    - To love God, is to obey God.

    - The enemy attacks through the mind in our thoughts, with the purpose of leading people away from God. Our flesh is guilty of the same.

    - Every time a sinful thought comes to mind, we need to bring our thoughts under control (captive) and seek to be obedient to God.

    - Will obeying God make us spiritually stronger? YES!

7. ***SEPARATION*** – **Ephesians 5:11 And have no fellowship with the unfruitful works of darkness,** but rather reprove [them].

- **1 Thessalonians 5:22 Abstain** from all appearance of evil.
- We must hate the sin but love the sinner.
- We must separate from sinners when they are involved in their sinful behavior.
- We must change our playgrounds, playmates, and playthings, then run to God.
- When we separate from sin, we must then cleave unto God.
- Will separation from sin make us spiritually stronger? YES!!!

8. *WITNESSING* - Mark 16:15 And he said unto them, Go ye into all the world, and **preach the gospel to every creature**.

- **Luke 10:2** Therefore said he unto them, the harvest truly is great, **but the labourers are few**: pray ye therefore the Lord of the harvest, that he would **send forth labourers** into his harvest.
- Everyone needs to hear the message of salvation.
- God has called us to go out and deliver that message.
- There are not enough laborers, so we need to step it up.
- Will witnessing make us spiritually stronger? YES!!

9. *FASTING* - Matthew 17:21 Howbeit **this kind goeth not out but by prayer and fasting**.

- You can pray without fasting, but you cannot fast without praying.
- Fasting is to deny the flesh and increase the Spirit.
- Denying the flesh means, bringing the flesh under subjection (under control).
- If a person can deny themselves from something that they need to survive, it will be that much easier to deny themselves of something unclean that they do not need to survive.
- Some of the biggest challenges can only be dealt with by prayer and fasting.
- Will fasting make us spiritually stronger? YES!

10. *GIVING/TITHING* Hebrews 7:4 Now consider how great this man [was], unto whom even the patriarch **Abraham gave the tenth of the spoils.** 5 And verily they that are of the sons of Levi, who receive the office of the priesthood, **have a commandment to take tithes of the people according to the law,** that is, of their brethren, though they come out of the loins of Abraham:

- **Malachi 3:8** Will a man rob God? Yet ye have robbed me. But ye say, **Wherein have we robbed thee? In tithes and offerings.** 9 Ye are cursed with a curse: for ye have robbed me, even this whole nation. **10 Bring ye all the tithes into the storehouse**, that there may be meat in mine house, and **prove me now herewith,** saith the LORD of hosts, if I will not open you the windows of heaven, and **pour you out a blessing, that there shall not be room enough to receive it.**

- God gives a challenge. He says try me! See what I will do, **if** you will be faithful to me in **giving**. God desperately WANTS to bless us! You can never out-give God.

- Financial giving is required by God, to be considered faithful. The Bible gives examples of how much to give to the church with the suggestion of a tithe or tenth. That would be a minimum of 10% of your income for the tithe.

- The suggestion that I have been taught for the offering is 5% of a person's income or half of what the tithe would be. That would make suggested giving to be 15% for both tithe and offering.

- **1Timothy 5:17** Let the elders that rule well be counted worthy of double honour, **especially they who labour in the word and doctrine.** 18 For the scripture saith, Thou shalt not muzzle the ox that treadeth out the corn. And, **the labourer is worthy of his reward.**

- The 10% tithe is suggested to go to the pastor for his service to the church, and the 5% offering is for paying the financial responsibilities of the church.

- The Pastor is considered the Elder. Those that labor in the Word deserve respect and double honor. The Pastor/Elder is worthy to receive financially from the church, for their great labor of love in the Church. Pastoring is a lot of work!!!

- The Bible is clear that giving is required by God. Christians should be glad to give because we love God, and because God has been so good to us.

Lesson 4 WALKING IN THE SPIRIT

- Without the support of the church members, the Pastor would not only have to be financially responsible for his own needs but also the needs of the church.

- An effective and healthy Pastor pours his heart out to the church and its members. It is reasonable for those same people that benefit from the church and its efforts, to financially invest in that ministry.

- Many churches do not bring in enough money to support the church and the Pastor. Those Pastors usually just take the giving/tithe that would go to them and give it to the church to take care of the church's financial responsibilities. Then that Pastor would have to get a job to provide for his family. They are considered bi-vocational Pastors.

- **2 Corinthians 9:6** But this I say, He which **soweth sparingly shall reap also sparingly**; and he which **soweth bountifully shall reap also bountifully** 7 Every man according as he purposeth in his heart, so let him give; not grudgingly, or of necessity: for **God loveth a cheerful giver**. 8 And God [is] able to make all grace abound toward you; **that ye, always having all sufficiency in all [things], may abound to every good work:**

- God wants you to be excited about giving to the Pastor and the church. God calls it robbery of God, to not be a giver (*Malachi 3*).

- Although we do not give with the mindset of getting in return, we are going to be blessed by God for our giving.

- God will **ALWAYS** provide for those that follow Him, according to His Word. Therefore, we need to give with the right attitude, and not be stingy or cheap with God.

- Why did God give an indication of what to give, and why give a range by using the term tenth? The fact is, God knows most people would not give much, without a clear indication of how much to give.

- Most people would cleave to the oneness doctrine in relation to their giving, meaning to put a "one-dollar bill" in the offering every week.

- Giving, the way God says to give, leads to blessings from God. Giving is also connected to the worship of God. Giving as God requires is a form of worship and obedience.

- Will giving in tithes and offerings make us spiritually stronger? YES!

CONCLUSION

- If we choose to walk in the Spirit, we can be sin-free. We need to seek perfection in our walk with God.

- God's definition of being perfect is not to be without mistakes.

- There were many men in the Bible who were called perfect but made huge mistakes. The people who were used the most by God were the people who made the biggest mistakes. Mistakes make a person wiser, and those mistakes are a training ground for maturity.

- God's definition of being perfect is, repenting perfectly.

- We cannot live in the Spirit unless we walk in the Spirit.

- We live in the righteousness of God when we walk and live in the Spirit

Lesson 5
TRUTH (Part 1)

There is only one salvation message, and we must obey it. No one had, or has, the authority to change that message. It is now clear, after the previous lessons, that the teachings in most churches today are different than what the Bible dictates. If you ask almost anyone who calls themselves a Christian how a person gets saved, they will tell you to accept the Lord as your personal Savior and you are saved. The most common tool used to introduce people to this untrue doctrine of salvation is to have people say what is called "the sinner's prayer." The problem is, a person can't be saved just by making a statement. A person can't be saved with taking some action on their belief, and there are no scriptures that mention a sinner's prayer.

There are actions that a person needs to take in order to be saved. Those actions are not the works of man, but the works of God. There are works of God that are required according to **Acts 2** and **James 2**; **Acts 2:40** *And with many other words did he testify and exhort, saying, Save yourselves from this untoward generation.* **James 2:18** *Yea, a man may say, Thou hast faith, and I have works:* ***shew me thy faith without thy works, and I will shew thee my faith by my works****.* We will go through **James 2:14-24** thoroughly in lesson 6. Those passages in **James 2** will support the idea of taking the necessary actions after someone believes.

There can be **no salvation without Jesus**, but we **must obey** Him to be saved. That is the only way you can save yourself. There is a "Truth", and if we follow the Word with consistency, we will see that Truth clearly *(2 Timothy 2:15)*. Again, those works are found in **Acts 2:38**. There is no other way to enter Salvation. This is not my idea or my revelation. It is revelation from scripture. Let's see what the Lord says about it, in His word.

1. **1 Corinthians 4:16 Wherefore I beseech you, be ye followers of me.** 17 For this cause have I sent unto you Timotheus, who is my beloved son, and faithful in the Lord, who shall bring you into remembrance of **my ways which be in Christ, as I teach everywhere in every church.**

   - Paul and Timothy taught that same **Acts 2:38** message to **everyone in every church**. We need to teach that same message today, everywhere in every church!

   - **There are not multiple ways to be saved.** Therefore, if people or organizations, have different teachings on how a person is to be saved, they need to repent and follow the Truth as it is written in the word of God.

2. **2 Timothy 2:15 Study to shew thyself approved unto God**, a workman that needeth not to be ashamed, rightly dividing the word of truth.

   - Truth, simply means to be right or accurate.

   - We must do what is accurate to be approved by God. We are to seek his acceptance; we don't accept him.

   - The way we become accurate is to study the Word of God and follow it. Denying **Acts 2:38** salvation is not following the Word.

3. **John 17:17** Sanctify them through thy truth: **thy word is truth**. 19 And for their sakes I sanctify myself, **that they also might be sanctified through the truth**.

   - Truth comes from the Bible. **We all have access to Truth**, so we have no excuse. (*Romans 1:20*)

   - We enter into sanctification (*becoming holy, or more spiritually mature*) over time. This is the product of Truth. Without Truth there is a lack of growth and maturity.

   - The Truth leads to walking in the Spirit. The Truth leads to salvation, and that is why the Truth will set you free *(John 8:31-32)*.

4. **Malachi 2:6 The law of truth was in his mouth**, and **iniquity was not found** in his lips: he **walked** with me **in peace and equity** and **did turn many away from iniquity**.

   - The scripture relates Truth to repentance.

   - If Truth is in you, iniquity, or sin, is not.

   - Truth brings peace and equity and the ability to be used of God in service to him.

   - If a person is full of iniquity, or sin, then the Truth is not in them.

5. **John 3:21** But he that **doeth truth cometh to the light**, that his deeds may be made manifest, that they are wrought in God.

   - Truth is related to an action, and that action brings the light.

   - Our actions tell us who we are in Jesus.

Lesson 5 TRUTH (Part 1)

- If a person is not doing what Jesus said, then Jesus is not in them. **Luke 6:46** *"And why call ye me, Lord, Lord, and do not the things which I say?"* **Matthew 7:21** *Not everyone that saith unto me, Lord, Lord, shall enter into the kingdom of heaven; but he that doeth the will of my Father which is in heaven. 23 And then will I profess unto them,* **I never knew you***: depart from me, ye that* **work iniquity**.

- How does a person engage Truth? How do we do what Jesus says? Repent, be baptized, and receive the Baptism of the Holy Ghost, and then walk in the Spirit!

6. **Jude 1:3** Beloved, when I gave all diligence to **write unto you of the common salvation,** it was needful for me to write unto you, and exhort you that ye should earnestly contend for the faith which **was once delivered unto the saints.**

- Common salvation means there are not multiple ways to be saved.

- No one has the authority to offer alternate ways of salvation. **Galatians 1:8** *But though we, or an angel from heaven,* **preach any other gospel** *unto you than that which we have preached unto you,* **let him be accursed**.

- We need to fight to restore and preserve that common salvation provided in **Acts 2:38** and throughout the rest of the book of Acts.

I. THE REVELATION OF TRUTH

7. **Acts 2:21** And it shall come to pass, that whosoever **shall call on the name of the Lord shall be saved**. 22 Ye men of Israel, hear these words;

- Peter is speaking to the Jews after they witnessed the 120 coming out of the upper room full of the **Holy Ghost and fire**.

- Peter takes this opportunity to preach. We know this because he said, "hear my voice." The topic of his message is salvation.

- From **Acts 2:23** to **Acts 2:35**, Peter preaches that Jesus is the Christ and this is summarized in *Acts 2:36 Therefore let all the house of Israel know assuredly, that* **God hath made that same Jesus, whom ye have crucified, both Lord and Christ.**

- The Jews responded, *"37 Now when they heard this, they were pricked in their heart,* **and said unto Peter and to the rest of the apostles, Men and brethren, what shall we do?"**

KINGDOM BIBLE STUDY SERIES

- It was clear that the **Jews** he was preaching to **believed** because they **felt conviction**. If they did not believe him, they would not have asked Peter what to do to be saved. The **Bible does not say** that **they were saved at that moment they believed** in their hearts and in their minds.

- Peter did not repeat the words, "call on the name of the Lord," to answer the question **"what shall we do?"**. However, whatever Peter answers is the definition of calling on the name of the Lord and leads them into salvation *(Acts 2:21)*.

- Peter answered their question in **Acts 2:38** with these words, "Then Peter said unto them, **Repent**, and **be baptized** every one of you in the name of Jesus Christ **for the remission of sins**, and ye shall **receive the gift of the Holy Ghost**."

- *"39 For the promise is unto you, and to your children, and to all that are afar off, even **as many as the Lord our God shall call**."* The direct promise is the Holy Ghost, and indirect promise is Salvation.

- Then the Word says, "those that **gladly received his word were baptized**," which would mean they were already repented. There would be no reason to baptize someone who was not repented.

- *"40 And with many other words did he testify and exhort, saying, **Save yourselves from this untoward generation**. 41 Then they that **gladly received his word were baptized**: and the same day there were added unto them about three thousand souls."*

- This passage calls for **action** to seek salvation. Verse 41 demonstrates that action was to be baptized, which would **demonstrate a person's belief or faith**. Conversely, you can say if a person is **not** water **baptized**, they **do not believe** as the scripture dictates.

- In these passages it **does not say the Jews received the Holy Ghost**, but we know they did. If they didn't receive the Holy Ghost, they would not be following Peter's directions, and they would not be able to be referred to as "saved" *(Romans 8:8-9)*.

- The verses other than verse 38, are often not emphasized in most churches, and this is true even among some Apostolic believers. **Verse 42 states a very important fact** that should be recognized.

- It says they continued and persevered in the doctrine of the apostles, which would include this teaching of **Acts 2:38**. In short, DON'T STOP TEACHING THIS DOCTRINE! *"42 And they **continued stedfastly in the apostles' doctrine** and fellowship, and in breaking of bread, and in prayers."*

Lesson 5 TRUTH (Part 1)

- Those who follow this doctrine call themselves **Apostolic Pentecostals.** That name comes from the fact that **the message was given on the day of Pentecost** by the **"apostle" Peter**. The doctrine is also referred to as **the "apostle's doctrine"**. **Apostolic** simply means relating to or teaching of the apostles.

- Verse 44 reinforces the idea that there are not multiple ways to be saved. There is only a common salvation, and the apostles agreed with Peter on what that common salvation message was. *"44 And **all that believed were together, and had all things common**;"*

- Verse 44 also perfectly concludes the point by stating, when the **people obeyed** the salvation plan of **Acts 2:38**, they were **characterized as believers**.

- A person does **not become a believer** because **of a thought or a statement**. A person becomes a believer because of the **willingness to "act"** on the Word of God. That is why this book is called the book of **"Acts" meaning the actions of the apostles.**

- Verse 46 tells us what happened next, which is they continued with the teachings of **Acts 2:38, all being in agreement**, acknowledging that **the message was from Jesus**. *"46 And they, **continuing daily with one accord** in the temple,".*

- That's what we need to do now. Continue daily in agreement with each other over this powerful salvation doctrine that is found in the book of Acts.

8. Acts 19:2 He said unto them, **have ye received the Holy Ghost since ye believed?** And they said unto him, we have not so much as heard whether there be any **Holy Ghost**.

- Many churches **believe** and teach that **a person receives the Holy Ghost the moment they believe**. This is **not the TRUTH!**

- According to this scripture, it is VERY clear that they were disciples, which means followers and believers. It is written that they believed, but they **did not** have the Holy Ghost.

- It is these kinds of errors that fill the **modern-day Christian doctrines** of salvation. Most people in churches today are being **taught incorrectly**, and it's hurting people spiritually all over the world.

II. THE HISTORY OF CHRISTIAN DOCTRINE

- If a person is saved by following the **Acts 2:38** plan of salvation, then where did the teaching of "Accept the Lord as your personal Savior," as a salvation plan come from?

- The apostles never taught anyone to be saved by accepting the Lord as their personal Savior, (*unless you define accepting the Lord as obeying* **Acts 2:38**).

- There are a series of events that have led to the teaching of the accept the Lord doctrine.

- One of these events is the development of the Roman Catholic Church.

- The question I would always ask myself was: How is there a Roman Catholic Church, when Romans killed Christians?

- The answer to that question led me to understand how the teaching of salvation changed in most churches today. It moved from **Acts 2:38**, switched to **Ephesians 2:8**, **Romans 10:9**, **John 3:16**, and any other scripture that mentions believing to be saved.

- The history of Christian doctrine is a very in-depth subject. We cannot give every detail of the multiple events that took place to develop Christian doctrine in this study. For more details and information, a good read is *The History of Christian Doctrine Volumes 1-3, written by Pastor David K. Bernard*. **Remember, consistently reading and studying legitimate spiritual material is an essential component of learning.**

- The following outline below will provide an abbreviated guide through some of the major events that led to the **Apostle's doctrine** being changed over time. We are going to start from the teaching of the apostles, move through history, and analyze where things went wrong.

Outline: History of Christian Doctrine

A. Apostles Teaching (Jesus Birth to 100 A.D.)

1. Discipleship was promoted heavily at this time.

2. Apostles taught repentance, baptism, and receiving the Holy Ghost.

3. This salvation message spreads because of its great power.

4. The last disciple, John the revelator, dies.

5. Satan ramps up his efforts to confuse the Apostolic teachings of the gospel.

Lesson 5 TRUTH (Part 1)

B. Constantine and Theodosius the Great. (200 to 1500's centuries A.D.)

1. Constantine was a Pagan Roman Emperor.

2. He was baptized on his death bed because he believed he could sin throughout his life, then have it washed at the end of his life. Not quite what Jesus had in mind.

3. Constantine showed acceptance and kindness to Christianity with the **Edict of Milan, written in 313 A.D.**

4. He influenced the development of the Roman Catholic Church (RCC).

5. The RCC was developed around the concepts of a Roman empire.

6. The Pope is like the emperor and acted similarly with his power and control.

7. The Pope, Bishops, and Cardinals gained power through **corruption.**

8. Constantine **tolerated Paganism** to keep the Roman Empire together.

9. His purpose was the cohesion of the empire and not the preservation of the Apostles doctrine of Jesus Christ.

10. **In 380 AD**, Roman Emperor Theodosius I issued the **Edict of Thessalonica** which made Christianity the official religion of the Roman Empire.

11. As the RCC developed, positions of power were bought and sold.

12. The Catholic Church adopted pagan and ungodly traditions.

13. Church services were taught in Latin to non-Latin speaking people.

14. Non-clergy was **not allowed to have Bibles.**

15. The practice of paying the RCC to have sins removed began **(1100's)**. They were called **indulgences**.

16. Sins like murder, divorce, and sexual immorality were forgiven by payments to the church.

17. Widespread corruption was the result of straying from the Word of God.

18. The RCC became so corrupt that there was a protest called **the Reformation (1500's).**

19. The actions of the RCC were historic in inappropriately reshaping the doctrines and teachings of Jesus.

20. This reshaping created doctrines and/or teachings that Jesus did not intend to be taught. They became false doctrines that are still being taught today.

21. There is still a form of indulgences being practiced today in the RCC called General Granting of Indulgences.

C. General Granting of Indulgences (Catholic Church today).

1. **Indulgences** are still practiced in the Catholic Church today: The Catechism of the Catholic Church describes an indulgence as "a remission before God of the temporal punishment due to sins whose guilt has already been forgiven, which the faithful Christian acquires through the action of the Church."

2. Basically, this means removing the consequences of past sins. **This is not biblical**. A person can have remission of sins, but the consequences of sin often last for years or may even be permanent.

3. Indulgences today are defined by this idea: You can "get" an indulgence for yourself, or for someone who is dead. You cannot "buy" indulgences anymore. The church **outlawed the sale of indulgences in 1567**.

4. This is a play on words. You can't get or pay for something that God forbids.

5. How a person can "get" an indulgence, today in the RCC, is by making charitable contributions, combined with other acts, that can help you "earn" and indulgence. There is a limit of one plenary (*absolute*) indulgence per sinner per day.

6. The way to earn partial indulgences is to follow the three "general grants" of indulgences. These are given for certain kinds of acts.

7. The first is to patiently go about your daily works and sufferings and pause to unite them to God through a short prayer. The Enchiridion (*indulgences prayers*) lists several ideas of what prayers one could say.

8. The second is to serve those in need with faith and mercy, such as providing for the poor.

9. The third is to voluntarily take on a penance of giving up some good things, such as fasting.

10. All these actions, when done devoutly and with God's love in our hearts, work to purify our hearts, according to the RCC.

11. There are no examples in the Bible of indulgences being practiced the way the RCC teaches or in any other way. An indulgence for a dead person is also foreign to the Word of God. This takes away free will from a person and the requirement to obey God while they are alive.

12. The practice of indulgences is false teaching and is contrary to the Word of God. A person is directed to live free of sin. If a person falls short, they are to repent.

13. Any sin that has taken place will be forgiven when repented of, but the consequences of sin remain. Therefore, this teaching of indulgences today is a false doctrine.

14. It is odd that Catholics would still be involved in this process, after all the harm and damage indulgences did to the church in early historical times. It is so important to resist sin if we want to avoid the extremely destructive and negative consequences of sin.

D. The Reformation – Birth of the Protestant Church (1500s A.D.)

1. A break from the RCC took place because of the corruption in the church.

2. The purpose was to get away from false teachings.

3. Those churches created outside the RCC were called Protestant churches because they were protesting the RCC.

4. Reformist leaders present a new and unbiblical revelation that **Ephesians 2:8-9** was the new salvation equation.

5. The "accept the Lord as your personal savior" path to salvation is born.

6. Anything a person would have to do to be saved is considered works.

7. **James 2:14-18, 22, 24**, that says that faith without works is dead, is ignored.

8. The Protestants become false teachers as well as the RCC.

9. This Transition and practice led to the complications we see in modern-day Christian churches today.

10. This appears to be the beginning of the great falling away of the church.
    2 Thessalonians 2:3 *Let no man deceive you by any means: **for that day shall not come, except there come a falling away first,** and that man of sin be revealed, the son of perdition;*

E. John Calvin and Martin Luther

1. **John Calvin** was a reformist leader that had a great influence on the reshaping of the modern-day Christian doctrine.

2. **John Calvin** believed, "Complete perfection is unattainable in this life, and the believer **should expect a continual struggle against sin.**" This mindset is only a half-truth.

3. This is a defeatist mentality that does not encourage repentance. We are supposed to expect victory in Jesus. This mindset has led to the modern-day teaching of "Christians are sinners and we sin every day."

4. Yes, **we sin "if" we are not walking in the Spirit**, but if we **walk in the Spirit, we will not sin** or fulfill the lust of the flesh. (*Galatians 5:16*)

5. We should strive against sin with everything we have. *Hebrews 12:4 Ye have **not yet resisted unto blood, striving against sin**.* This will lead to more repentance and less sin, and eventually, with practice, a sin-free life.

6. **Calvin originally** defined salvation as, "**the acceptance by** which **God regards us as righteous** when a person has been **received into grace**." This statement would mean that **God accepts us**, and **we become righteous** when **in his grace**. This is true, but overtime the reasoning and logic of Calvin, and mankind as a whole, changed this truth into **people accepting God,** instead of **God accepting us**.

7. **Calvin** became **devoted to** the subject of **justification by faith alone**, using the scripture in **Ephesians 2:8** as his text. However, Ephesians was written by the apostle Paul to a church that had already been established on the **Acts 2:38** salvation.

8. **Salvation by faith alone** began to spread and the idea of **acceptance of the Lord** ushered in the "accept the Lord as your personal savior" method of salvation. **This was not the message taught by Jesus, the Apostles, or even the Catholic Church**.

9. **No one has the authority to add a new salvation plan** to the one that was already established by Jesus and distributed by the Apostles.

10. **Martin Luther** was a RCC monk in 1505. He posted 99 articles to the church door, which was the way to challenge the RCC and its practices at that time. To do so would have meant certain death, so his followers physically removed him from the area. Luther wanted to stay and confront the RCC religious leaders with their wrongdoings. This would have been a fatal decision.

11. **Martin Luther** went on to start the Lutheran Church. It was very similar to the RCC but Luther made some adjustments such as eliminating indulgences. **Like John Calvin, Luther also focused on being saved by grace** (*Ephesians 2:8-10*).

12. **Luther argued that every good work designed to attract God's favor is a sin.** "God's grace, which cannot be earned, alone can **make them just**." **He appears to be saying that doing things to try to please God is sin.** Seeking **to please God is called obedience.** Clearly, **obedience** to God **is not a sin**.

13. To say that it is a sin to attract the favor of God by a good work **is biblically unheard of.** What **"Works"** is all about will be elaborated **in Lesson 6** in the section called "**What Is Believing, Faith, and Works**".

14. **Luther** wrote: "**Be a sinner, and let your sins be strong,** but let your trust in Christ be stronger, and rejoice in Christ who is the victor over sin, death, and the world. We will commit sins while we are here, **for this life is not a place where justice resides."** This would mean there is no righteousness here on earth. Not true.

15. This idea **promotes and accepts sin** in a Christian's life. We are not sinners when we are repented. "**Be a sinner and let your sin be strong**" is a **biblical contradiction**. However, **this mindset would please Satan** very much. The research reveals that **Calvin** also believed a person could sin and laugh in the devil's face. This was because Satan couldn't get you even while that person is living in sin.

16. The fact is, **this thinking** was **planted by Satan into the minds of these men**. This is an anti-Christ mentality. These ideas are the product of reasoning that is not consistent with scripture, and **false teaching leading to more false teachings.**

17. It is not clear why Martin Luther would want to make a statement like this after he left the RCC because of its unbiblical practices.

18. Calvin and Luther's teachings and reasoning radically changed Christian theology. They had come to **believe that people are saved through faith alone (belief or thoughts)**, and not through their own acts of obedience to the Word of God.

19. These **changes to the doctrines** of Jesus are the **origin of the modern-day Christianity.** This "accept the Lord" teaching of Salvation, is taught in the majority of the Protestant churches today. Protestant churches are considered all non-Catholic churches.

20. This false teaching has **drastically deviated** from the Salvation message delivered by the apostle Peter in the book of **Acts chapter 2 verse 38**.

21. **Catholic churches** do not teach the **Act 2:38** plan of salvation either. This is odd because the Catholic Church believes that **the apostle Peter was the first Pope!** I am not sure why they would not obey Peter's message.

22. **Anyone proclaiming Christianity** needs to make sure they have **entered the gospel** of Jesus Christ by **repenting** of sin, **putting on Jesus** by getting **baptized** in the name of Jesus (*Galatians 3:27*), and obeying and submitting to the Spirit of God by **receiving the baptism of the Holy Ghost** (*Romans 8:8-9*).

CONCLUSION

So, **where did the accept the Lord as your personal savior** plan of salvation **come from**? Answer, approximately 500 years ago Christian Reformists attempted to get away from the RCC by following a new revelation of being saved by faith and grace alone. Those Reformists also came to believe that sin was a natural part of a Christian's life. Not following the scripture left those individuals with less spiritual knowledge and power. This caused more sin in their lives because of the false teachings that were established.

Instead of fixing the problem through repentance and rightly dividing the Word of Truth (*2Timothy 2:15*), people proclaiming Christianity, continued going further and deeper into false teaching. Therefore, most churches today are teaching the "accept the Lord" equation for salvation. **How do we fix it?** Those of the reformation, and the other Protestant Churches that came out of the reformation, did not go back far enough in history to fix the problem. They attempted to fix the errors of the RCC, but did not go back to the teaching of the apostles. **Restoring the Acts 2:38 salvation message is the answer.**

Ironically, I was doing a study on Baptism with a friend of mine and I found some research from a person who was a Lutheran. This person stated that Lutherans of today do not clearly depict what Luther believed back in his time. **The Lutheran writer found that even Martin Luther believed that Baptism was required for salvation and that it washed away sin.** Luther just hated the idea that "mankind" could have anything to do with its own salvation. This deeply disturbed Luther.

This caused Luther to lean towards eliminating man from any involvement in the salvation plan. This was accomplished by teaching that Salvation comes ONLY through God's grace, by the Faith a person has in God. This statement is true, however it's only the broad picture of salvation. The specific and detailed process is **a person acts in Works of Faith**, and because of **God's grace they are saved**. Which simply means, **we are saved even though we don't deserve it**. We are saved because he loves us. In lesson 6 we will **outline specifically how Works of Faith works.**

Luther's logical mind was battling with what the word said compared to how he was feeling about it. That is his first mistake. **Even though his heart felt that what the apostles taught was true, his logical mind led him away from his heart.** This led him deeper and deeper into teaching false doctrine. As the centuries passed, this false doctrine was passed down from generation to generation and had a devastating effect on the Truth of the gospel of Jesus Christ.

The Truth matters! A passenger airplane has 600,000 moving parts. If only 1% of those moving parts do not work, that would mean 6,000 moving parts are not working. Would you get on a plane that had 6,000 moving parts that did not work? That plane is destined to crash. If we are involved with doctrines that are not accurate, our spiritual lives are bound to crash. Even if the doctrine is 99% correct, that 1% matters. That 1% could get us in trouble and even keep people out of Heaven. **The previous lessons show us exactly how to do what the reformers should have done, which is to go back to the basics.**

KINGDOM BIBLE STUDY SERIES

Lesson 6
TRUTH (Part 2)

(Presenting Truth to The Masses)

After centuries of transformation, the teachings of salvation would be unrecognizable and unacceptable to Jesus and the apostles. So how does a person know what is right or wrong in relation to the doctrines being taught today? The good news is the word is able to prove itself. Anytime a study is going to be done in the word of God, on any subject, one of the most important things that needs to happen, to maintain truth, is **reconciliation**. This is defined as the action of **making one view or belief compatible with another**.

The Bible does not contradict itself. Therefore, if two scriptures on the same subject appear to say different or opposite statements, those **scriptures must be reconciled**. Many people from opposing viewpoints of a scripture will respond with the mindset "you have your interpretation and I have mine". However, the scripture says in *2Peter1:20 Knowing this first, that no prophecy of the scripture is of any private interpretation. 21 For the prophecy came not in old time by the will of man: but holy men of God spake as they were moved by the Holy Ghost.* This means people can't say they have their own interpretation and be in line with the word of God. The very next verse says in *2 Peter 2:1 But **there were false prophets also among the people**, even as there shall **be false teachers among you**, who privily shall **bring in damnable heresies**, even **denying the Lord** that bought them, and **bring upon themselves swift destruction**. 2 And many shall follow their pernicious ways; by reason of whom the way of **truth shall be evil spoken of**.*

This helps us understand the importance of reconciling scriptures. If we do not do so consistently, the result will be false teachers, teaching false doctrine, that causes them and the people they teach to deny Jesus. This leads to destruction, and the Truth will be called false or heresy. **Anyone proclaiming to be a Christian should want to make sure they are in Truth and in turn teaching Truth. To do anything less is to deny Jesus.** Nothing good can come out of denying Jesus. The reason why truth is referred to as evil, is when **people have learned a false doctrine, and when Truth is presented to them, it is foreign to them.** This is because it doesn't match **their theology** (*study of the nature of God and religious belief*). The only way to **get beyond this problem** is to analyze the **scriptures** to make sure they **reconcile with each other**. Then the **Truth will be made manifest**, and everybody wins.

Below we will investigate various teachings and analyze the modern-day Christian belief system. Then we will use scriptures from the Apostolic mindset and attempt reconcile them. This is how we will get to the Truth. **We will begin with the idea that a person is saved when they have faith alone or believe.** This comes from the **modern-day Christian theology. Every time the scripture mentions believing, in relation to salvation, it's referring to believing in Repentance, Baptism, and receiving the Holy Ghost.** This is the **Apostolic theology.**

Any teaching of the Bible must be consistent with the rest of scripture. **Here is what the scripture says about what it is to believe.** The 3 components of **Acts 2:38** are all connected to believing in the following passages. **This is another way to prove that a person demonstrates that they believe by obeying** the Apostolic doctrine of salvation found in **Acts 2:38**.

1. **Mark 1:15** And saying, the time is fulfilled, and the kingdom of God is at hand: **repent ye and believe the gospel**.

2. **Mark 16:16** He that **believeth and is baptized shall be saved**; but he that believeth not shall be damned.

In both scriptures, **Repentance and Baptism are directly connected to belief.** The word "and" is an adjoining word. **That means more than believing is required for salvation.** If all you have to do is believe to be saved, there would be no "and" in either of these passages.

Therefore, **if a person does not Repent or get baptized, they cannot say they believe according to the scripture**. It is clear, if this is true of Repentance and Baptism, it must also be true of the Holy Ghost. If a person does not have the Holy Ghost, they do not belong to Jesus (*Romans 8:9*), and therefore they don't believe. The following passage also links the Holy Ghost to believing.

3. **John 7:37** In the last day, that great [day] of the feast, **Jesus stood and cried**, saying, if any man thirst, let him come unto me, and drink. **38 He that believeth on me, as the scripture hath said**, out of his belly shall flow rivers of living water. 39 But this **spake he of the Spirit** (*Strong's 4151, Pneuma in the Greek*), which **they that believe on him should receive**: for **the Holy Ghost** (*Strong's 4151, Pneuma in the Greek*) was not yet [given]; because that Jesus was not yet glorified.

- If a person **believes**, they will have living water flow from their belly. Then, Jesus clarifies that the living water is the Spirit/Holy Ghost, that had not yet been given. Jesus goes on to say that when He is glorified, the Holy Ghost will be given, and people will be able to receive it. Both Spirit and Holy Ghost are the same Greek word.

- The word says it clearly. If a person **believes** in Jesus as the Word says, they will receive the Holy Ghost. The opposite is also true. If a person **doesn't believe**, they will not, and cannot, receive the Holy Ghost.

- **Therefore, anytime the Word mentions believing or faith, in relation to salvation, it must include Repentance, Baptism, and the Holy Ghost.** Therefore, it is correct to say a person is saved by faith or saved when they believe. However, it must be clarified that faith or belief must be followed by action to be activated and legitimate. In short, **don't just believe, but activate your faith.**

- **The modern-day Christian** mindset is partially correct. But details matter. When any scripture that mentions belief or faith is mentioned in the word, **Mark 1:15, Mark 16:16,** and **John 7:37-39** give **the Apostolic details** of what believing is scripturally. **This is how the two thoughts are reconciled. This is how we know that Acts 2:38 as a salvation plan is the Truth.**

I. THE BIBLE UNDERSTANDING OF Believing, Faith, AND Works.

What I am about to say will be foreign to a modern-day Christian. **I will, easily and biblically, reconcile every verse.** Then it will make perfect sense. When this lesson is finished there will be no contradictions to contend with. That is why it is the **Truth**. **The only question will be, will you follow and obey the Word?**

A person needs to have **faith,** which is to **believe**, and needs to act on that belief. To act on a belief is **works**, then a person can be **saved**. We have already established that those, actions or **works, are to Repent, be water Baptized, and receive the Holy Ghost.**

Those that have been indoctrinated **into modern-day Christianity, believe that a person is not saved by works.** They believe people are saved by grace through faith alone. **There are scriptures that say Works is not a part of your salvation and there are scriptures that says Works is a part of our salvation.** Since we know that the Bible does not contradict itself, we must reconcile those verses. First, we are going to define the terms, and then reconcile then scriptures.

A. Believe - 4100 πιστεύω pisteuo [pist-yoo'-o], to think to be true, to be persuaded of.

- The Greek translation shows that to **believe means that you have come to understand that something is true**. It does not mean that any action was taken on that understanding. It does not mean that action is automatically taken place as a result of a thought.

Lesson 6 TRUTH (Part 2)

B. Faith - 4102 πίστις pistis [pis'-tis] - In the NT of a conviction or belief.

- **Faith and belief are almost identical.** The word belief is used in the definition of Faith. The Greek words are also very similar. **Both faith and believe are also used synonymously with salvation in the Word of God.** *(Acts 1:21, Acts 13:48, Acts 18:27, Galatians 2:16, Galatians 3:6, Ephesians 1:13, Romans 4:3, Ephesian 2:8-10).*

4. **Romans 10:16** But they **have not all obeyed** the gospel. For Esaias saith, Lord, **who hath believed** our report? 17 So then **faith [cometh] by hearing**, and **hearing by the word** of God.

    - **If you don't hear the gospel, you can't obey the gospel.** There were many who were not in obedience to what the apostles were teaching. The same is true today. **When a person believes** (*or has faith*) **in what God says in his word, they will be obedient.**

    - **This obedience is directly connected to faith. If you don't obey, you don't have faith** (*or believe*). Also, obedience is directly connected to action. So, faith and action are also connected. **If a person does not act on what the Word says, then you don't have faith.**

5. **James 1:21** Wherefore lay apart all filthiness and superfluity of naughtiness, and **receiven** with meekness **the engrafted word, which is able to save your souls.** 22 But **be ye doers** of the word, and **not hearers only, deceiving your own selves.**

    - **Faith comes by hearing the word.** Then the **person/hearer** is biblically **required to be a doer of the** Word after he or she hears the Word. **This would be an act/work of faith.** Obeying the Word to commit an act/Work of Faith determines that the individual **Believes**.

C. Works - 2041 ἔργον Ergon [er'-gon] AV-work 152, deed 22, doing 1, labour, an act, deed, thing done:

- **Works** is different from **belief** and **faith**, as it concerns a deed or action, and not just a thought, feeling, or conviction. What a person does after a thought, feeling, or conviction is Works.

- **Works** is associated with both **being a part of salvation, and not being part of salvation** in the Word of God.

Since the Bible does not contradict itself, we know that there must be two kinds of **works**. The Bible will demonstrate that there are **works of man** and **works of faith,** and those **works of faith** are found in the **book of Acts**. This understanding will reconcile the opposing thoughts of **works** and salvation.

Every verse we evaluate must be reconciled with what we have already determined in the word of God. We will now put the verses used by modern-day Christianity into context with what was already established by the apostles. This is how we come to the knowledge of **Truth.**

6. **Ephesians 2:8 For by grace are ye saved through faith**; and that not of yourselves: it is the gift of God: 9 **Not of works, lest any man should boast.** 10 For we are his workmanship, created in Christ Jesus unto **good works**, which God hath before ordained that we should walk in them.

   - We are saved by grace, which is the unmerited favor of God. We must have faith to enter His grace and salvation. **That verse is meant to be broad and not specific**. The specifics of being saved by grace is found in **Act 2:38-42**. It's by His grace we can enter into His salvation, even when we don't deserve it. **A person is not saved by a thought.**

   - The same Greek word **2041 Ergon [er'-gon]** -Work, deed, doing, labor, an act, deed, thing done: **Not of works** is clearly describing deeds or **works of man**. The verse is saying mankind, has not and cannot, provided the opportunity for salvation.

   - **Ephesians 2:8-10** is **not saying don't obey the book of Acts** salvation plan. This book **was written by the apostle Paul** to the Ephesians who had already **established the church** in Ephesus **on the Acts 2:38** salvation plan. **The very plan Paul was saved by in the book of Acts.**

   - A person cannot do enough good deeds or give enough donations to earn salvation.

   - It is biblically accurate to say that the **works of man** cannot save you.

   - Can you save yourself? The answer is **Yes** and **No**.

   - You cannot save yourself without the plan of salvation from Jesus.

   - You can save yourself from this untoward generation. **Acts 2:40** And with many other words did he testify and exhort, saying, **Save yourselves from this untoward generation**. This is done **through obedience** to **Act 2:38**, which are **Acts of Faith**.

7. **Galatians 2:16** Knowing that a **man is not justified by the works** of the law, **but by the faith of Jesus Christ**, even **we have believed in Jesus Christ**, that **we might be justified by the faith of Christ**, and **not by the works** of the law: for **by the works** of the law shall **no flesh be justified.**

- The same Greek word 2041 **Ergon [er'-gon] -Work, deed**, doing, labor, an act, deed, thing done:

- The distinction here is the words **works of the law**. This simply means **deeds or acts** required by the **law of Moses**.

- As mentioned earlier, **faith** and **believing** are used synonymously, and both lead to being justified in Jesus Christ. **Justified** 1344 dikaioo [dik-ah-yo'-o] 1342;- justify, be freed, to be righteous. Justified means saved.

- Ultimately, a person is not saved by the **works of man**, but a person is saved by **acts of faith** found in the **book of Acts**. A person is saved when they **believe** and **act on that belief.**

- This passage is **not suggesting** that **works is defined as** Repenting, getting Baptized or receiving the Holy Ghost, as modern-day Christians would have you believe.

8. **Galatians 3:1 O foolish Galatians, who hath bewitched you, that ye should not obey the truth,** before whose eyes **Jesus Christ** hath been evidently **set forth**, crucified among you? 2 This only would I learn of you, **Received ye the Spirit by the works of the law**, or by the **hearing of faith**? 3 **Are ye so foolish**.

11 But that **no man is justified by the law** in the sight of God, [it is] evident: for, **the just shall live by faith. 12 And the law is not of faith**: but, **the man** that **doeth them shall live in them**.

- A person is not obeying the **Truth** if they rely on the works of the law instead of Jesus. As in **Galatians 2**, this is referring to **deeds** or **works of man** from the **law of Moses**.

- If a person is deceived to believe in the Works of the law instead of the works of faith in Jesus, then they are foolish!!!

- This passage is not suggesting that **works** is Repenting, getting Baptized or receiving the Holy Ghost, as modern-day Christians would have you believe.

- Paul established the Galatian church the same way he set up the church in Ephesus. There are not two ways to be saved. As we saw earlier Paul taught the same thing in every church everywhere he went (*1Corinthians 4:17 For this cause have I sent unto you Timotheus, who is my beloved son, and faithful in the Lord, who shall **bring you into remembrance of my ways** which be **in Christ, as I teach every where in every church**.*)

Here are a few more scriptures that heavily emphasize that **works** is not a part of the salvation plan.

9. **2 Timothy 1:9** Who **hath saved us**, and **called [us]** with an holy calling, **not according to our works**, but **according to his own purpose and grace**, which was given us in Christ Jesus before the world began,

10. **Romans 11:6** And if **by grace**, then [is it] **no more of works: otherwise grace is no more grace**. But **if [it be] of works, then is it no more grace**: otherwise work is no more work.

- All those passages seem to make it clear that **works** isn't part of our salvation. Just to review, most modern-day Christians believe that Repentance, Baptism, and Receiving the Holy Ghost are **works**. **According to them**, a plan of salvation that included **any actions a person must take to be saved would be considered works**, and therefore not biblical.

11. **Romans 4:2** For **if Abraham were justified by works**, he hath [whereof] to glory; but **not before God**. 3 For what saith the scripture? **Abraham believed God, and it was counted unto him for righteousness.**

- The modern-day Christian church suggests that these passages prove, that all a person must do to be saved is **believe**. This would mean **once a person is persuaded** that Jesus is their savior, **they are saved**.

- **Romans 4** says that **Abraham** was **not justified** by **works**. He was saved because he **believed**, and it was considered by God **as righteous** (*referring to Genesis 15:6*).

The Truth is the three actions in **Acts 2:38** is **works**. However, once again, there are two kinds of works, **works of man and works of faith**. **Works of Man** is not related to salvation and **works of faith** is related to salvation. Now it's time to present the scriptures that reveal that there is a **works of faith**.

12. James 2:20 But wilt thou know, O vain man, that **faith without works is dead**? 21 Was not **Abraham our father justified by works, when he had offered Isaac his son upon the altar**? 22 Seest thou how **faith wrought with his works, and by works was faith made perfect**?

23 And the scripture was fulfilled which saith, **Abraham believed God**, and **it was imputed unto him for righteousness**: and he was called the Friend of God. 24 **Ye see then how that by works a man is justified, and not by faith only.**

- This appears to be a **direct contradiction** in the word of God. **Romans 4** specifically says that **Abraham was not justified by works**, and **James 2:21** says **Abraham was justified by works and works made his faith perfect**?

- The same Greek word is used for **"work"** in both passages. 2041 ἔργον Ergon [er'-gon] AV-work 152, deed 22, doing 1, labour, an act, deed, thing done: This proves there are **deeds or actions that don't justify** or save people, and **there are deeds or actions that do save people.**

- Since we know that it is impossible for the Bible to contradict itself, we must reconcile these passages. All that needs to be done is turn "Faith without works", into **Faith and works together**, hence the term **works of faith**. This is how we **reconcile** that there are **two different kinds of works!**

- The first part of **Romans 4:2** is referring to **works of man**, and the second part is referring to **works of faith**. **James 2:21** is referring to **works of faith**.

- **Romans 4:3** says that Abraham **Believed** God and it was counted to him as righteousness. **His belief was demonstrated by action! James 2:21-22** establishes the **work of faith** that Abraham did to show that he **believed** God (*Genesis 22:1-19*).

- When **Abraham believed God**, this was a demonstration of **his faith**. What were the **works or actions** of his **faith?** The willingness **to sacrifice his son.** This can be established because we know assuredly that **Romans 4:3** and **James 2:22-23** use the same words to describe the actions of the same man (*Abraham*). **That is classic reconciliation!**

- If Abraham wasn't willing to sacrifice his son, he would be **demonstrating unbelief**. This would have **led him to be unrighteous**. His **action, or act of obedience,** was the **evidence of his belief**. It was the same when he was commanded to be circumcised and circumcise all his house.

- In *Genesis 15:6 And he believed in the LORD; and he counted it to him for righteousness.*, **Abraham** was described as a person who **believed and was righteous**. In **Genesis 17:10-14**, he was told **if he didn't obey** the act of circumcision, **he would be cut off**. He would also be seen as **breaking a covenant** with God.

- **Abraham was righteous before** the command of circumcision, but **without obeying** the act or **works of faith** of circumcision, **he could not remain a believer**. It is the same with the command of Repentance, Baptism, and receiving the Holy Ghost.

- If a person **does not submit** to the command to do all three, then that person **is not a believer**. This may sound harsh, but this study has already proven that all three of these **works of Faith** are directly **related to believing**.

13. Galatians 3:6 Even as Abraham believed God, and it was accounted to him for righteousness.

- In this verse, the same is said about Abraham believing God. Now we can rightly divide the word and understand what **Galatians 3:6** is saying. It **wasn't** that Abraham **believed in his mind**, but he **believed with his actions**.

- Again, this passage is referring to the fact that Abraham was willing to sacrifice his son out of his **faith** towards God. Therefore, his **righteousness was a result of his works of faith which was described as believing**.

This is how scripture is reconciled. The best way to make sure that a **scripture is taught in context**, is to look at the **scriptures before and after** a scripture that is presented. When this is done with **James 2:14,17-18**, and **25-26**, it **will continue to reinforce what we have already discovered**. Just for teaching purposes we will also go over **James 2:20-22** again as well. **Repetition is one of the most productive ways to learn.**

14. James 2:14 What doth it profit, my brethren, though a man say he hath faith, and have not works? Can faith save him?

- This is a question that directly identifies the subject of this passage as **faith** and **works**. The scriptures that follow are going to clearly answer that question.

- I believe that God already knew that modern-day Christians were going to wrongfully declare that salvation comes through faith alone (*mental thought or declaration*).

- Therefore, we can look at the following passages as God providing a way to correct that mind set, which is a false teaching (*false Doctrine*).

- God is going to answer the question "can faith save without works", further along in the text.

15. James 2:17 Even so faith, if it hath not works, is dead, being alone. 18 Yea, a man may say, thou hast faith, and I have works: **shew me thy faith without thy works, and I will shew thee my faith by my works.**

- Now we know that **believing** without **works of faith** is useless, lifeless, spiritually dead (*Strong's definition of "dead"*). The emphasis is magnified by specifying that faith is demonstrated by works, meaning:

16. James 2:20 But wilt thou know, O vain man, that faith without works is dead? 21 Was not **Abraham our father justified by works**, when he had offered Isaac his son upon the altar? **22 Seest thou how faith wrought with his works, and by works was faith made perfect?**

- The passage starts by calling those that didn't understand, foolish. There is a repetition of the simple fact that **faith** without works is dead. This means a person **cannot be saved** if they believe (*have faith*), **without acting** on that belief.

- It even gives a more descriptive concept of **works making faith perfect! Works and faith are connected!** Again, if Abraham would **not have been willing** to take the action of sacrificing his son (*Works*), then Abraham would not be considered a man with faith.

- Since **works** in these passages are connected to salvation (*verse 14 and 23*), we can classify them as **works of faith**. A person must have Faith that God will **forgive them** when they repent, have Faith that God **will wash away their sins** in Baptism, and have Faith that God will **fill them with the Holy Ghost.**

- It requires **faith** because you can't see the sin being forgiven or washed, and you can't see the Holy Ghost enter a person's body. A person **must have faith** that God will do these things that the Word says He will do.

17. James 2:23 And the scripture was fulfilled which saith, Abraham believed God, and it **was imputed unto him for righteousness**: and he was called the Friend of God. 24 Ye see then how that **by works a man is justified**, and not by **faith only**.

- There are those who believe that James and Paul disagreed and had opposing teachings. This is impossible if you believe that the **word is infallible**, and you believe that both men were **inspired by the same Spirit** (*the Spirit of God or the Holy Ghost*).

KINGDOM BIBLE STUDY SERIES

- For James and Paul not to agree, would that mean **the Holy Ghost wasn't in agreement with itself?** This doesn't make any sense, and that is why I believe **James 2:20** calls those who didn't understand, foolish. Remember, in **2Peter 1:20**, the word makes it clear that **the Holy Ghost wrote the Bible through men of God.**

- This passage determines that the other verses that use the same wording (*Romans 4:2 and Galatians 3:6*), **must be reconciled** with **James 2:23**, as it adds a completely different meaning than the other two scriptures despite the usage of the same words. To do so, is to understand that **Romans 4:2** and **Galatians 3:6** both means the same thing as **James 2:23.**

- The **Truth** is both **Romans 4:2** and **Galatian 3:6** are saying that belief is not a mental thought, but belief is an action that requires **works of faith**. When the **actions** required by God are **completed**, then a **person can say they believe**. Those saving actions have been clearly shown throughout this lesson, and throughout the whole KBS (*Acts 2:38*).

- We know that **works of faith** are essential because that is what is **stated and repeated**, over and over in **James 2:14-26**.

- **James 2:24** gives the answer to the question in verse **James 2:14**. The answer is NO! **Faith** alone cannot save you. It is impossible that verse 14 is referring to **works of man**, as the subject is salvation. The Word has already established that **works of man** is **not related to salvation**.

- **James 2:24** clearly states that **works of faith is a part of salvation** by the usage of the word **"justified"** (*made righteous, saved*). It should be obvious by now that the **justifying works** in the Bible is found in **Acts 2:38**.

- This determines that the "**accept the Lord as your personal Savior,**" "**saved by faith or mental belief alone,**" or the saved by the "**sinners prayer,**" plans of salvation **cannot be true** or accurate. **Those doctrines are not righteous, nor can they produce righteousness.**

- The only way a person could be **saved by faith alone,** is if that **faith** was defined as **believing** and **obeying the gospel** message of **Acts 2:38** and included **continuing to do good** deeds throughout life (*walking in the Spirit, Galatians 5:16*).

- "**Faith without works is dead**" speaks for itself. The scripture is telling us that the **works of Faith** determines what kind of **faith** a person has in God.

Lesson 6 TRUTH (Part 2)

- **Abraham was justified by works and faith together.** This means the definition of "believing" is the combination of **works by faith**. **Believing** that brings salvation is defined by the components of **Acts 2:38** (*Works of Faith*).

18. James 2:25 Likewise also was not **Rahab the harlot justified by works**, when she had received the messengers, and had sent [them] out another way?

19. Hebrews 11: 31 By faith the harlot Rahab perished not with them that believed not, when she had received the spies with peace.

- The terms "justified by works", and "By faith", are also used synonymously in relation to Rahab in those passages in **James 2** and **Hebrews 11**. This proves that **justifying works** (*or saving Works*) is the same as **having faith**. Since justified means saved, this would equate to **works of faith** that leads to salvation.

20. James 2:26 For as **the body without the spirit is dead**, so **faith without works is dead also.**

- If it hasn't been repeatedly stated clear enough, the **Word** gets even more specific. This description is designed to get people to picture what the body is like without the spirit. The **Truth** is the **body CANNOT exist without the spirit**.

- The Word is making it clear that **faith also CANNOT exist** without the **works of faith** that must accompany it.

21. Ephesians 1:12 That we should be to the praise of his glory, who first trusted in Christ.**13** In whom ye also [trusted], after that ye heard the **word of truth, the gospel of your salvation:** in whom also **after that ye believed, ye were sealed with that holy Spirit** of promise,

- There is a **Truth** that comes from the **Word** of God. The gospel is the good news that we can be saved **if we follow** the directions given by the Word.

- The usage of the words "after that ye have believed", means after a person **has obeyed the directions to the gospel message** (*Act 2:38*), they **will be sealed** and **obtain the promise**. This means they will be **saved**.

22. 2 Thessalonians 2:12 That **they all might be damned who believed not the truth**, but had pleasure in unrighteousness.

- We have thoroughly discussed what it means to **believe the Truth**. This passage shows us what happens when people **refuse to believe the Truth, they will be Damned**. It is blunt and very scary. That is **why we need to listen** to it. This is another reason we need to buy the Truth and sell it not (*Proverbs 23:23*).

The Word has proven, unequivocally, that Repentance, water Baptism, and receiving the Holy Ghost are all directly connected to what it is to be a **believer**. If a person has not engaged or entered all three, then that person cannot legitimately claim to be a **believer**. **This is the Truth!** This **Truth** was established **because we reconciled the scriptures** to make sure they were understood in context with each other. Not doing so would create false doctrine. **Unfortunately, false doctrine has dominated the modern-day non-denominational protestant churches of today.**

Again, the **Truth** is anytime the scripture instructs a person to **Believe**, regarding salvation, it clearly means to believe in **Repentance, Baptism, and receiving the Holy Ghost** (*Acts 2:38*). This is where the **New Testament Gospel salvation message is delivered**.

To **teach any other gospel of salvation** is a contradiction to the Word and will **bring a curse** on people (*Galatians 1:8*). If a person lives life as a great person, goes to church their whole lives, prays and reads their Bible every day, gives their tithes, and does good things for people. They still cannot make heaven their home unless they follow the **True biblical salvation plan.**

This can be said with all boldness and confidence after all the evidence has been presented in the previous lessons from the Word of God. It's time to further evaluate the **Works of Faith** a person must do to be saved.

II. WORKS OF FAITH IN SALVATION

Works of man is attempting to earn your way into salvation by doing good deeds. **Works of faith** is submitting to the commandments of God by obeying, by faith, the spiritual things He expects us to do in order to be saved. The Bible clarifies in James 2, that a person shows their Faith by their **works**. Here are three most prevalent **works of faith** that are connected to salvation. I am sure you will not be surprised by what they are.

- **Repentance** is a **work of faith**: When a person repents, they must have **Faith** that God forgives them of their sin. We cannot see the forgiveness happening, that's why it's of **faith**. We can see the fruits of repentance (*Matthew 3:8 and Luke 3:8*). **Repentance is not a work of man because a man cannot forgive you of your sins** (regardless of what happens in the Catholic Church/Confession). *Acts 26:20 But shewed first unto them of Damascus, and at Jerusalem, and throughout all the coasts of Judaea, and [then] to the Gentiles, **that they should repent and turn to God, and do works meet for repentance.***

- **Water Baptism** is a **work of faith**: People cannot see the sin being washed away in baptism, nor can they see the blood of Jesus that is washing the sin. A person submits to getting baptized and then they have Faith that God will do the part He promised to do, which is remission of sins. *Colossians 2:11 In whom also ye are circumcised with the circumcision made without hands, in putting off the body of the sins of the flesh by the circumcision of Christ: 12 Buried with him in baptism, wherein also ye are risen with him through the **faith of the operation of God**, who hath raised him from the dead. 13 And you, being dead in your sins and the uncircumcision of your flesh, hath he quickened together with him, **having forgiven you all trespasses**;* **This is not a Work of Man because a regular man cannot remit, or wash away your sins.**

- **Receiving the Holy Ghost** is a **work of faith:** You cannot see white smoke, mist, or anything enter a person's body as you receive the baptism of the Holy Ghost. What happens is a person begins to worship and believes God can fill them with His Spirit. The initial evidence that a person receives the Holy Ghost, is the evidence of speaking in tongues. After receiving the Holy Ghost, a person should demonstrate the fruits of the Spirit (*Galatians 5:22-25*). A person must have faith that God will do His part, which is filling the person with the Holy Ghost. **This is not a work of man because a man cannot fill people** with the **Holy Ghost**, only Jesus can.

- **Walking in the Spirit,** according to **Galatians 5:16**, is a **work of faith**: The Word says if you will walk in the Spirit then you will not fulfill the lust of the flesh. We have Faith that we can be free of sin, and as a result, we are prepared for the rapture (*catching away of the church*). This is a **work of faith** that will give us the ability to maintain our repentance. **This is not a work of man because man cannot walk in the Spirit by their flesh** (*Romans 8:5-8*).

III. THE MODERN-DAY CHRISTIANITY SALVATION MESSAGE

Christianity is one of the largest religious belief systems in the world. Most of these Christian churches believe in salvation through accepting the Lord as their personal Savior. I have been referring to this group of Christians as "modern-day Christians" or "modern-day Christianity." We have well established in the Word of God, that this teaching is a false teaching (false doctrine), that was passed down from historical figures of our past.

The belief in the **Acts 2:38** salvation plan is in the vast minority, and it has been so throughout history. When everyone is going in one direction, and a small group of people stop and go another way, it looks like that small group is going the wrong way. Just because most people are going in one direction, does not mean that direction is the right one. As a matter of fact, the scripture specifically mentions this in *Matthew 7:13 Enter ye in at the strait gate: for wide is the gate, and broad is the way, that leadeth to destruction, and many there be which go in thereat: 14 Because strait is the gate, and narrow is the way, which leadeth unto life, and few there be that find it.* The wide gate/way is the large group, and the straight or narrow gate/way is the smaller group that goes in another direction. The many end up in destruction and the few, or those on the road less traveled, end up with life. **If we want to spread life, we must make sure that the salvation message we teach is the message that Jesus intended and approves of.**

The way to stay on the straight and narrow is to evaluate the scriptures used by the modern-day Christian groups and show how those scriptures are consistent with Acts 2:38. The most common scriptures used to describe how salvation takes place within Modern-Day Christianity are found in **John 3:16**, **Ephesians 2:6** and, **Romans 10:8-9**. **Unfortunately, for those teaching these doctrines, salvation is declared, by most, without true repentance, the necessity of water baptism for the remission of sins, and the filling of the Holy Ghost.** Most of the time, these steps may be entertained after they have declared a person as saved. However, the focus is on Faith and Faith alone. We have already established that this teaching is inconsistent with the other scriptures that relate to salvation.

Either modern-day Christianity is wrong, or the Bible is wrong. **Well, we know that the Bible is not wrong.** Therefore, this Bible study has been designed to enlighten anyone interested in getting back to consistency with the Word of God in relation to the salvation message. It is also for those who are **not afraid to question religion for the sake of Truth**. We are going to review **John 3:16**, **Ephesians 2:6** and, **Romans 10:8-9** to determine if they can be reconciled with **Acts 2:38**.

23. John 3:15 That **whosoever believeth in him should not perish** but have eternal life. 16 For God so loved the world, that he gave his only begotten Son, that **whosoever believeth in him should not perish**, but have everlasting life. 17 For God sent not his Son into the world to condemn the world; but that the **world through him might be saved**. 18 **He that believeth on him is not condemned**: but he that **believeth not** is **condemned** already **because he hath not believed** in the name of the only begotten Son of God.

- Believing in Jesus does bring a person to salvation. Does believing mean knowing in your mind and heart that Jesus is Lord? The answer is NO! Not by itself. **Believing is determined by action or works of faith.**

- The Word establishes that to Believe in Jesus is to repent and believe (*Mark 1:15*), believe and be baptized (*Mark 16:16*), and Believe as the scripture has said which is to receive the Spirit/Holy Ghost (*John 7:38*). If you don't receive the Spirit, you are not Believing Jesus as the scripture hath said. If you do not have the Spirit, you are not His (*Romans 8:9*).

- Every time "believe" is mentioned in the Bible in relation to salvation, **there is no way to separate it from the books of Mark chapters 1 and 16, John chapter 7, and James chapter 2.** To "Believe" **is not a mere acknowledgement** of the fact that Jesus is our Savior.

- It is impossible that the Word was suggesting that the acknowledgement of Jesus saves us because this would be contradictory to the other scriptures.

24. Ephesians 2: 8 For by grace are ye saved through faith; and that not of yourselves: the gift of God: 9 **Not of works**, lest any **man should boast**. 10 For we are his workmanship, **created in Christ Jesus unto good works**, which God hath before **ordained that we should walk in them.**

- Again, grace is the idea that **we do not deserve salvation**, but **we have the opportunity** to enter into salvation because of God's favor. **Faith is a person's system of belief.**

- Faith is the fervent **conviction** that God exists, according to the Greek word Pistis (*pis'-tis),* in the Strong's Concordance. **A conviction is essential in a Christian's life, but a conviction alone does not save a person.**

- In the book of **Acts 2:37**, Peter was preaching to the Jews, and they became **convicted**. That conviction led to them asking what they needed to do to be saved. Then they did what they were told, and they were described as saved. **Therefore, our convictions must lead to action to be effective.**

- Faith in what? Faith in Repentance, Baptism, and Receiving the Holy Ghost. This is how we are **"Saved through faith."**

25. Romans 10:1 Brethren, my heart's desire and prayer to God for Israel is, that they **might be saved**. 2 For I bear them record that they **have a zeal of God**, but **not according to knowledge**. 3 For they being ignorant of God's righteousness, and going about to **establish their own righteousness, have not submitted themselves unto the righteousness of God**. 4 For Christ *is* the end of the law for righteousness **to every one that believeth**.

- Verse 1 shows that this letter is written to a backslidden Israel, who were not walking in line with God. **Romans 10:21** confirms this idea, *21 But to Israel he saith, All day long I have stretched forth my hands unto a disobedient and gainsaying people*.

- The apostle Paul was not trying to tell gentiles of today how to be saved in Romans 10. It was an attempt to **reach out to Israel** because **they were lost** and needed Jesus.

- **It appears that the Jews** Paul is writing to in the book of Romans chapter 10, **were attempting to hold on to the old Jewish traditions like circumcision. They were also attempting to keep the law of Moses** (*Acts 15:1, 24*).

- Paul desired that Israel would be saved. They were on fire for God, but they **were not knowledgeable** about the things of God. As a result, they did not understand **God's righteousness and established their own ways, which was not God's ways.**

- In most modern-day Christian churches, if not all of them, **Romans 10:9** is described as **the scripture that shows a person how to get saved. Clearly, this is not the Truth.** We should be careful not to make the same mistake the Jews made.

- We should take this passage as a warning to make sure that we **understand Romans 10:9 according to knowledge and the righteousness of God**, and not establish something that was not intended by God.

Romans 10:9 That if thou shalt **confess with thy mouth** the Lord Jesus, and **shalt believe in thine heart that God hath raised him from the dead, thou shalt be saved.** 10 For with **the heart man believeth** unto righteousness; and with the **mouth confession is made unto salvation.** 11 For the scripture saith, whosoever believeth on him shall not be ashamed.

- The first thing we must establish is that the book of Romans was an Epistle, which means a letter to the church. **Those churches, in all the Epistles from Romans to Jude, were established on the Acts 2:38 salvation message.**

Lesson 6 TRUTH (Part 2)

- The next important detail to remember is, **Romans 10:9** is directed to a backslidden Israel, and **what THEY need to do to repent of their self-reliance.**

- **Paul would not be sending the church in Rome a letter to change the plan of salvation. No one had the authority to change the salvation plan** the church was already established on, **not even Paul.**

- It must also be recognized that **Romans 1:20-32**, speaks of **the need for Repentance. Romans 6:1-23 deals with Repentance** and **Water Baptism**, and **Romans 8:1-10** deals with **Repentance and the Holy Ghost.**

- It is **not an educated practice, theologically,** to **skip Romans 1-9, jump** to **Romans 10**, and then proclaim that a person is saved when they obey verse 9. **That is taking the Word of God out of context.**

- In **Romans 10:9**, the **directive was for the Israelites** to **recognize and confess the authority of Jesus.** Then by **Faith declare that Jesus is God** and their redeemer. **If the Jews did so, they would be saved.** They were lost and needed to turn to Jesus.

- Confession is not just using words. Faith without works is dead! **Israel needed to Repent! If they were backslidden, they could be grafted back in. If they had never entered the gospel, they needed Believe.** This would lead to acting on the salvation plan that Paul delivered to Rome (*Acts 2:38*).

- Confessing the Lord Jesus is **done verbally first, and action must immediately follow.** If there was no repentance by the Jews, the **Jews would not be confessing Jesus as Lord.** They would **not be demonstrating belief from the heart.**

- Verse 11 mentions that if we Believe, we won't be ashamed. That is because when you have **demonstrated belief through action**, then you **have obeyed God.**

- **God's word was not being followed**, even though **Israel had a zeal** (*excitement*) **for God.** As a result, the Jews were overcome with doctrines that **are not of knowledge.** It established the **righteousness of man and religion**, and **not the righteousness of God.**

- The same would be true **of any group of people who try to establish their own way of seeking salvation. This is exactly what is happening** in the modern-day Christian churches of today. The salvation **message has been changed** to "accept the Lord as your personal savior". This is **not Truth.**

- The True message is to believe in Jesus. This means to follow the plan He provided through the apostle Peter. *Matthew 16:18 And I say also unto thee, That thou art Peter, and **upon this rock I will build my church**; and the gates of hell shall not prevail against it. **19 And I will give unto thee the keys of the kingdom of heaven**.*

- Peter built that church in the book of Acts when he preached the first message of New Testament salvation.

Romans 10:13 For whosoever shall call upon the name of the Lord shall be saved. 14 How then shall they call on him in whom they have not believed? and how shall they believe in him of whom they have not heard? and how **shall they hear without a preacher? 16 But they have not all obeyed the gospel.** For Esaias saith, Lord, who hath believed our report? **17 So then faith cometh by hearing, and hearing by the word of God.**

- The Israelites were being directed to **call on Jesus and believe**. Then they were told how, which is to **hear the preacher and obey the gospel**. The purpose **was to get them away from** the distractions of **the law Moses**.

- It is likely that the Israelites were **mixing and matching both** the teachings of **Paul** and the **law of Moses**. This would not be acceptable to Jesus.

Verse 13 – In lesson 5, Truth Part 1, we already established the **definition of "calling on the name of the Lord"** in *Acts 2:21 And it shall come to pass, that whosoever shall call on the name of the Lord shall be saved. 22 Ye men of Israel, hear these words;.*

- **Acts 2:21** and **Romans 10:13** both use the words **"Calling on the name of the Lord"**. If **Acts 2:21** is defined as Repent, Baptism in the name of Jesus Christ for the remission of sins and be filled with the gift of the Holy Ghost, then so is **Romans 10:13**! **This is another classic example of reconciliation of the Word of God.**

- **Romans 10** is all about Jesus Christ and His salvation plan. **Since there is only one plan of salvation**, then whatever is said in **Romans 10 about salvation, must be reconciled with the Acts 2:38 plan of salvation.** This is exactly what we have done.

- If a person misses this connection between **Romans 10:13** and **Acts 2:21**, **Romans 10:2** tells us why. **The painful truth is that the person is unlearned.** They are not operating in God's way but **establishing their own way**.

Lesson 6 TRUTH (Part 2)

- **The modern-day Christian departure from Truth** started **as far back as** the teaching of **the early church** in the book of Acts and **continued to the time when the Reformists** separated from the Catholic Church in the 1500's (*John Calvin and Martin Luther*). **This departure continues today.**

- **Upon reading these lessons, our faith should be activated.** God is calling humanity to hear His Word. **Jesus desires** for **people to make** the necessary **adjustments** to **establish themselves in God**, and **not in their own beliefs**. Establishing one's own beliefs is what causes religion. **The Word of God is all we need to fix any errors that may have come from man-made religion.**

- The 3 modern-day believing scriptures used by the modern-day Christian church (*John 3:16, Ephesians 2:8-10 and, Romans 10:8-9*), contradict the 3 **true believing scriptures** (*Mark 1:15, Mark 16:16, John 7:38-39*), used by the Apostolic church, **in relation to what it is to be saved according to the Bible.**

- A person cannot say that **they have called on** him **if they have not believed**. If a person does not repent, get baptized, and receive the Holy Ghost, **then they have not called on Him.**

- What we have just accomplished, is giving **every person who may have been indoctrinated** in the "accept the Lord" doctrine of salvation, the ability to scripturally **release that teaching, and enter God's righteousness**.

- There have been only two ways to be saved in the Bible. The Old Testament Salvation and the New Testament Salvation. The Old Testament has been fulfilled by the New Testament and **the New Testament is a better Testament** (*Hebrews 7:22*).

The **Acts 2:38** salvation plan does not contradict **Ephesians 2:8-10**, **John 3:16**, or **Romans 10:9-10**. It fulfills them! Now that we have reconciled these passages, we can now see that they are consistent with **Acts 2:38**.

IV. TAKING EVERY PASSAGE IN THE WORD OF GOD LITERALLY

Is it possible for a person to be misled or misread the Word and get it wrong? What causes such a mistake to happen? What happens to a person who makes this mistake? What should a person do if they end up making this kind of mistake? There are **several scriptures** in the Word of God, **that are not intended to be taken literally**. If this happens, the result will be the creation of false doctrine. Below are some examples of how this might happen.

KINGDOM BIBLE STUDY SERIES

26. 2 Peter 3:16 As also in all *his* epistles, **speaking in them** of these things; in which are **some things hard to be understood**, which **they that are unlearned and unstable wrest, as** *they do* **also the other scriptures, unto their own destruction**. 17 Ye therefore, beloved, seeing ye know *these things* before, **beware lest ye also, being led away with the error of the wicked, fall from your own stedfastness. 18** But **grow in grace**, and *in* **the knowledge** of our Lord and Saviour Jesus Christ. To him *be* glory both now and for ever. Amen.

- The Bible is not always as direct as we wish it were. We must take the Word line upon line, precept upon precept (*Isaiah 28:13*), **to get** what Jesus wants us to get, **and be** what He wants us to be.

- As we have mentioned before, if two scriptures involving salvation appear to contradict each other, and two people have different interpretations of what they mean, **we must find the answer.** We can't just say, "Well, you have your interpretation and I have mine" (*2 Peter 1:20*), and both people be ok with God!

- One will be in Truth and the other will be in False Doctrine. One will be saved and the other will not be, until he or she **makes the necessary adjustments** to adhere to the Word of God. Then they can be saved! Unfortunately, **there is no way around this.**

- Let's answer the questions listed above. **Yes, it is possible for someone to be misled or misread the scripture.** It is well established in the Word of God that there are false teachers who teach false doctrine. **2 Peter 2:1** *But there were* **false prophets** *also among the people, even as there shall be* **false teachers** *among you, who privily shall bring in* **damnable heresies***, even* **denying the Lord** *that bought them, and bring upon* **themselves swift destruction***.*

- This is because some Bible subjects are more difficult to understand than others and require more study. What a person needs to do when they have been misled or have misunderstood a passage, is first accept the fact that not every scripture is to be taken literally. Then do what it says in verse 18, which is to **grow in grace and knowledge of Jesus Christ.**

- Here are some more examples of scriptures that should not be taken literally.

27. Hebrews 6:4 For it is impossible for those who were once enlightened, and have tasted of the heavenly gift, and were made partakers of the Holy Ghost, 5 And have tasted the good Word of God, and the powers of the world to come, 6 **If they shall fall away, to renew them again unto repentance**; seeing they crucify to themselves the Son of God afresh, and put him to an open shame.

- It appears to say that if a person falls away in sin, they can never repent. That doesn't seem to make sense if you know the Bible. **We are taught we can repent if we sin**. The Bible says we have an advocate with the father if we sin.

- I can't be 100% certain I know the answer, but it seems that it is either referring to the **unforgivable sin being committed**, which the Bible says cannot be repented of, or the sin the person commits has them in a mindset to **completely denounce Jesus**. If a person is in that mindset, they would not be able to repent.

28. Hebrews 6:9 But, beloved, **we are persuaded better things of you,** and things that **accompany salvation**, though we thus speak. 10 **For God is not unrighteous to forget your work** and labour of love, which ye have shewed toward his name, in that ye have ministered to the saints, and do minister. 11 And we desire that every one of you do **shew the same diligence to the full assurance of hope unto the end**: 12 That ye be not slothful, **but followers of them who** through faith and patience **inherit the promises.**

- This passage seems to be making a distinction between the person who cannot repent in **verses 4-6**, and the servants of God in verses **9-12**. When saying "better things of you", it seems to say that there are two types of people being spoken of: **One that is willing to serve God and one that once had an experience with God, but then denounces God.**

- The one who cannot repent, is the one who has committed the unforgivable sin or has completely denounced Jesus. The one who inherits the promise, is the one that works for God and has faith.

- What it **cannot be saying** is that **a person who lives for God and makes a mistake, or sins, can never repent**. This would directly contradict the Word of God.

29. 1 John 2:1 My little children, these things write I unto you, that ye sin not. **And if any man sin, we have an advocate with the Father**, Jesus Christ the righteous: 2 And **he is the propitiation for our sins**: and not for ours only, but also for the sins of the whole world.

- This passage determines that if a person sins, they can repent because **the Father is their advocate**. Since the Bible does not contradict itself, we simply must use this knowledge to understand that **Hebrews 6:4 is not saying what it appears to say.**

- Even if the meaning of **Hebrews 6:4** is not 100% clear, what is 100% clear is what it is not saying. **It is not saying a person can never repent after having an experience with God**, and we have scripture to back that up.

- Ironically, **1John 2:1** is also a scripture that proves that **1John 3:9 cannot be taken literally.**

30. 1 John 3:9 Whosoever is born of God **doth not commit sin**; for his seed remaineth in him: and **he cannot sin**, because he is born of God.

- For this passage to be taught by itself without including the other scriptures around it, would be **taking it completely out of context.** This passage is not to be taken literally, by itself.

- What it appears to mean is while a person is in the state of being a child of God, **the person doesn't sin because of the Holy Ghost within them** (*a person cannot be a child of God without the Holy Ghost*).

- However, when a person is tempted and then sins, the **Holy Ghost cannot remain** in that body, and we are not complete in Jesus. **The Bible says the Spirit and the flesh cannot reside together** (*Romans 8:7-9*).

- King David asked God to not take the Holy Spirit from him when he sinned. **Psalms 15:11** *Cast me not away from thy presence; **and take not thy holy spirit from me**.* Which proves the Spirit could be taken from him because of his sin.

- The Bible teaches us that **sin separates us from God** (*Isaiah 59:2*), and we cannot go to heaven if we die un-repented *(1Corinthians 6:9-11)*. We get these warnings in the Word, because people who get saved can end up in sin if they don't walk in the Spirit.

- The NIV says it this way in *1 John 3:9 No one who is born of God **will continue to sin**, because God's seed remains in them; **they cannot go on sinning**, because they have been born of God.* When stated in this way, it does not contradict scripture. This translation seems to be clearer.

- We know what **1John 3:9** isn't saying. In 1John 2:1, it clearly shows that a person can sin. Therefore, **1John 3:9 cannot be taken literally**.

- I have had a man in my office once, banging on the desk, insisting that this passage was 100% literal. However, there are many scriptures that refer to the ability of a fallen man to be regenerated. As a result, **it would be an unlearned teaching** to say a Christian could not sin at all, ever.

Lesson 6 TRUTH (Part 2)

31. Romans chapter 7:1 Know ye not, brethren, for I speak to them that know the law, **how that the law hath dominion** over a man as long as he liveth? 2 For the woman which hath an husband **is bound by the law** to *her* husband so long as he liveth; but if the husband be dead, she is loosed from **the law of *her* husband**. 3 So then if, **while *her* husband liveth, she be married to another** man, **she shall be called an adulteress**: but if her **husband be dead, she is free from that law**; so that she is no adulteress, though she be married to another man.

I heard a well-known Apostolic preacher, whom I will not name, preach on YouTube that a woman who divorces her husband, after he commits adultery, is still an adulteress and a whore, if she gets remarried while her ex-husband is alive. He preached the same would be true of the man. **Romans 7:1-3** was the passage he used to support his proclamation. I knew from my previous studies that this did not seem correct, and it bothered me that what he was saying appeared to be true in the Word. So, I began to study it further. Very quickly the answer would be revealed in the very next verse.

4 Wherefore, my brethren, ye also are become dead to the law by the body of Christ; that **ye should be married to** another, even to **him who is raised from the dead,** that we should bring forth fruit unto God. 5 For when we were in the flesh, the motions of sins, which were by the law, did work in our members to bring forth fruit unto death. **6 But now we are delivered from the law**, that being dead wherein we were held; **that we should serve in newness of spirit, and not in the oldness of the letter.**

- We must be careful teaching out of the Word of God **without taking the scripture in context.** As stated earlier, the best way to stay in context is to **read the whole chapter**, or at the very least, **the verse before and after** the verse in question.

- In this case, verse 4 reveals that when we enter the New Testament, **we are no longer under the law but under Christ.** Therefore, the comments about being in adultery if you remarry while your spouse is **still alive refers to the Old Testament times and does not carry into the New Testament.**

- But wait! **In Mark chapter 10**, it says if a spouse remarries, they are in adultery. *"10 And in the house his disciples asked him again of the same matter. 11 And he saith unto them, Whosoever* **shall put away his wife, and marry another, committeth adultery** *against her. 12 And if a woman shall put away her husband, and be married to another, she committeth adultery."*

- It also says the same thing in *Luke 16:18 Whosoever putteth away his wife, and marrieth another, committeth adultery: and whosoever marrieth her that is put away from her husband committeth adultery.*

- **Well, then it must be true? It says it three times.** This is when study and understanding are essential. It protects us from false teaching and heresy!

- **Matthew chapter 5** and chapter **19** will give us the answer.

32. **Matthew 5:32** But I say unto you, that whosoever shall put away his wife, **saving for the cause of fornication**, causeth her to commit adultery: and whosoever shall marry her that is divorced committeth adultery.

33. **Matthew 19:9** And I say unto you, whosoever shall **put away his wife, except** *it be* **for fornication**, and **shall marry another, committeth adultery**: and whoso marrieth her which is put away doth commit adultery.

- In the books of **Mark** and **Luke**, there is **no mention of any exception to the rule** if fornication is involved.

- But with further investigation, we find that in Matthew, it tells us twice, fourteen chapters apart, that **there is an exception of infidelity that determines you can remarry if your former spouse is still alive.** According to Matthew, this can be done without committing adultery.

- As a result of what is stated in **Matthew 5** and **19**, a precedent is set for the passages in both Mark and Luke as well. **Simply put, if it is true in Matthew, it is true in all the gospels because the Bible does not contradict itself.**

- If there is scriptural backing to an argument, **it doesn't matter how true something looks** in some passages. If the Word says something isn't true, then it just isn't true. **The Word is the authority**, not the person trying to explain it.

- That pastor on YouTube REALLY believed what he was preaching, and he preached it hard. But he was REALLY wrong. Why? Because he could not recognize that what he was preaching **was inconsistent with scripture**. He didn't see what he was suggesting could not be true, because **it contradicted scripture**.

- In **Romans 10:9,** it REALLY looks like it's saying that all a person has to do is confess Jesus with their words, and believe in His resurrection in their heart, and they will be saved. However, just as the previous scriptures demonstrate, the whole context must be considered.

Lesson 6 TRUTH (Part 2)

- Since there are other scriptures that tell us how a person gets saved, we must make sure that **Romans 10:9** is consistent with them, too. There are several scriptures that state a person is saved when they believe, and these could be mistaken for scriptures that support **Romans 10:9** as a salvation plan. However, with careful consideration of the Word of God, we already know what it means to "believe" according to scripture. Therefore, **Romans 10:9** cannot be taken literally.

- We have already established that those **"believing to be saved passages", support the Acts 2:38 salvation plan**, if they are considered in context. When we did so earlier in this lesson, we were able to come to the determination that the statements in Romans 10 were intended to lead Israel to salvation, and **not the salvation as it is taught by the modern-day Christian groups.**

We have gone through great lengths, scripturally, to demonstrate how easy it is to misunderstand some passages of the Word of God. To be taught or teach something incorrectly, is **an unlearned person wrestling with the scripture to their own destruction.**

These statements are not an attempt to say that a person is dumb if they didn't know something correctly in the Word of God. The only thing that would make someone unwise, **is to not make the necessary corrections** based on the realization that there are errors in their beliefs or teachings. What would be **unwise, is to not receive the Truth**, that is so obviously presented in the Word of God, as a result of the **unwillingness to release previous teachings** (*indoctrination*). I have been in church 20 years, and there have been at least a half dozen things I thought were biblical and found out after more in-depth study that it was incorrect. When that happened, I made the necessary adjustments in my teaching. **What is most important, is that we learn.**

It is now very clear that it is a serious matter for a person who is claiming Christianity to be accurate, and in Truth, in a time **where there are so many incorrect teachings**. We have more access to the Word of God than ever before, so **we are responsible for what we receive as biblical teaching**, and **what we teach others**. We can't say, "Sorry God, I didn't know."

The good news is that the solution is quite simple. The **scripture gives us the answer**, and that is to **grow in grace and knowledge of our Lord Jesus.** (*2 Peter 3:18*) We must acknowledge that **we are not saved** by accepting the Lord as our personal Savior **without acting on that acceptance.** The **only way to accurately say** that a person is **saved by accepting the Lord** as their personal savior is to say that **the definition of accepting the Lord is Repenting, being Baptized and Receiving the Holy Ghost.** We must acknowledge that **Acts 2:38** is the only salvation plan. When a person does so, they will **find a deeper and more intimate relationship with Jesus.**

KINGDOM BIBLE STUDY SERIES

V. WHAT AM I SUPPOSED TO DO NOW?

So, what's next? Find a church that is teaching **Acts 2:38** salvation. Find a Pastor that you think you will be able to trust, to teach you this Truth. If you have been taught that you are a sinner and you sin every day, **embrace the idea that you can be free from sin every day** and fight to achieve it. If you have been baptized by sprinkling, or as an outward expression of an inward faith, or taught that baptism does not wash away your sins, **get re-baptized in the name of Jesus for the remission of your sins.** Re-baptism is a biblical principle (*Acts 19:1-7*). If you have not received the Holy Ghost evidence by speaking in tongues as the scripture has said, **ask someone with experience in praying for people through to the Holy Ghost, and have them pray with you to receive it. Submit to God and He WILL fill you.** He wants you to have the Holy Ghost more than you want it. Then, finally, **learn how to walk in the Spirit** and allow yourself to be used by God to **serve His kingdom**.

VI. THE PRODUCT OF UNBIBLICAL PRACTICES

You can NEVER go in the right direction taking the WRONG road. It is impossible. To go in the right direction, you have to take the right road. The Bible gives us some insight into this Truth.

34. Galatians 1:6 I marvel that ye are so soon removed from him that called you into the grace of Christ unto another gospel: 7 Which is not another; but there be some that trouble you, and would **pervert the gospel of Christ.**

- This scripture shows us that "another gospel" is one that looks like the gospel of Jesus, but it has been changed and perverted.

- Teaching that someone is saved by accepting the Lord as their personal Savior, is another gospel that, "is not another." It is perverted which is why it is considered false a doctrine.

35. Galatians 1:8 But though we, or an angel from heaven, **preach any other gospel unto you** than that which we have preached unto you, **let him be accursed.** 9 As we said before, so say I now again, if any man preach any other gospel unto you than that ye have received, let him be accursed.

- Teaching anything other than what **the Apostles taught**, and how they taught it, **will be cursed.**

Lesson 6 TRUTH (Part 2)

- Most church denominations say they have the **Truth**, and they preach out of the Bible, **but all of them do not rightly divide the Word of Truth**.

- The Bible warns us that this is going to happen and **says, "be accursed" twice** to demonstrate how serious this issue is.

36. Matthew 7:15 Beware of false prophets, which come to you in sheep's clothing, but inwardly they are ravening wolves.

37. Matthew 24:11 And many **false prophets** shall rise, and shall deceive many.

38. Matthew 24:24 For there shall arise **false Christs, and false prophets,** and shall shew great signs and wonders; insomuch that, **if it were possible,** they shall **deceive the very elect.**

39. Mark 13:22 For false Christs and false prophets shall rise, and shall shew signs and wonders, **to seduce**, if it were possible, even **the elect.**

40. 1John 4:1 Beloved, **believe not every spirit**, but try the spirits **whether they are of God**: because **many false prophets** are gone out into the world.

41. 2 Peter 2:1 But there were **false prophets** also among the people, even as there shall be **false teachers among you,** who privily shall **bring in damnable heresies**, even **denying the Lord** that bought them, and **bring upon themselves swift destruction.**

- Since the Bible greatly emphasizes the idea that there will be false teachings taught by false prophets, **shouldn't people take that warning seriously?**

- This warning should cause people to **be very cautious about what they have learned**, about God and the Bible. People should **seriously scrutinize** their knowledge and understanding when confronted with the idea that they **may have been taught false doctrine.**

42. Proverbs 23:23 Buy the truth, and sell it not; also wisdom, and instruction, and understanding.

- We need to be SOLD OUT to what the Word is truly teaching!

- We need to be sold out to **Acts 2:38** salvation, **freedom** from sin through **Repentance**, **Baptism** for the remission of sin as a part of our salvation, receiving the **Holy Ghost** evidenced by **speaking in tongues, walking in the Spirit**, and the **Oneness of God** (*Oneness will be taught in the KBS Volume 2 "Developing Christ in You"*). KBS Volume 3 will be called "Developing Christ in the Church."

43. 2 Thesselonians 2:10 And with all deceivableness of unrighteousness in them that perish; because they received not the love of the truth, that they might be saved. 11 And for this cause **God shall send them strong delusion, that they should believe a lie:**

- Those who **do not receive the love of Truth will perish** because they will be deceived and **trade in the Truth for a lie** (*false doctrine*).

- You WILL be saved **if you love the Truth**. If you do not love the Truth, God will send you a delusion to believe false teachings and **you will believe those false teachings are true.**

- **If a person believes they are in Truth and they are not, why would they seek the Truth?** They already think they have it. This study is designed to help expose false doctrine **so the Truth can be attained.**

44. 2 Thessalonians 2:12 That they all might **be damned who believed not the truth** but had pleasure in unrighteousness.

- You will not buy the Truth if you do not love the Truth.

- People who **enjoy their sin,** more than they love the Truth, **will be damned.**

- If you **do not believe** the Truth, **you will not be saved.**

- Once you are born again, **seek Truth** with all your heart, and the **Holy Ghost will lead you to all Truth** (*John 16:13*).

CONCLUSION

- There are scriptures that show the true meaning of what it is **to believe**, and **have faith**, in relation **to salvation**.

- There is a **works of man** and a **works of faith**, and only one of them can save you.

- There is a **modern-day Christian church that means well**, but they are teaching false doctrine.

- Every scripture in the Bible cannot be taken literally. Doing so has caused many false teachings.

- Now that **Truth has been revealed**, seek out a church and Pastor, that is teaching this Truth. Then allow yourself to **learn and grow**.

- There is a consequence for not being responsible for what a person learns and teaches, from the Bible. **If it is false doctrine destruction will follow**.

- There is **a Truth**, seek it, love it, keep it, and pass it on!

Lesson 7
WISE AS A SERPENT AND HARMLESS AS A DOVE

(This Lesson is for Bible Study Teachers)

1. **Matthew 10:16** Behold, I send you forth as sheep in the midst of wolves: be ye therefore wise as serpents, and harmless as doves.

You will find that many people will have an adverse reaction to what the KBS is teaching. Most often, the reason is because **it doesn't match what they have been taught already**. It **doesn't meet their theology**. It's shocking and sometimes offensive to people who have had a long-time relationship with God, in the modern-day Christian church. **A teacher of Apostolic Truth can be right in doctrine and wrong in their approach and presentation.** Here are some tips to present this **Truth** without causing harm.

NOTE TO THE BIBLE STUDY TEACHER:

- **Never** attempt to **lead with the lessons on Truth**. Make sure you go through all the previous lessons before Truth, with some measure of success and understanding from your students. **Lessons may have to be repeated** before starting the lessons on **Truth**. This is perfectly normal and acceptable. **Become familiar with each lesson** before you teach it. You will be in danger of confusing people if you don't.

- Some teachers may feel like the person they are teaching has not been indoctrinated by any previous belief system, and they may not need to know all the details about the modern-day Christian church. They may feel like, "I'll just teach them salvation and skip the other lessons." **Keep in mind that knowing the other details, will protect the new convert from those who will try to teach them against this truth in the future.**

- When learning this material, the new convert will have even more reason to buy the truth and sell it not (*Proverbs 23:23*). With full knowledge of the modern-day Christian doctrines being taught today, your students should learn **how to convert other modern-day Christians** themselves **someday.**

Lesson 7 WISE AS A SERPENT AND HARMLESS AS A DOVE

- If a student tells you that all you must do to be saved is believe, or have faith, let them know the only difference between you and the student's mindset, is the definition of what it is to believe. Then keep teaching the lessons.

- A person who claims to be a Christian without having been Repented, Baptized, or has received the Holy Ghost, **should never be told they do not have God. They should never be told they do not have a relationship with God either**. This person may have a relationship with God, **just not the fullness of the relationship that Jesus wants** them to have.

- If a Bible teacher tries to take a person's God away from them, **you are going to have a fight on your hands. They may have a form of God**, but they just need more God. *2 Timothy 3:5 Having a form of godliness, but denying the power thereof:*

- Telling them they do not have God **will repel them from your Bible study, and they may never come back**. Simply search the scriptures together and ask God to direct your hearts.

- Only seek to teach those who want to learn, or at least want to have a reasonable and educated discussion about the Word. **If a person just wants to fight about scripture, let them go.** If they are denying the power of God, then it's ok to turn away and simply pray for them. *2 Timothy 3:5 Having a form of godliness, but denying the power thereof: **from such turn away**.*

- As I stated earlier, if a person does not have the Holy Ghost, it is more difficult to lead them to all truth. *John 16:13 Howbeit when he, **the Spirit of truth**, is come, **he will guide you into all truth**: for he shall not speak of himself; but whatsoever he shall hear, [that] shall he speak: and **he will shew you things to come**.*

- If there is a great deal of resistance from the person you are teaching, simply keep the focus on **Acts 2:38** salvation, and **especially seeking the Holy Ghost. Just keep meeting and teaching** with grace and mercy. Let God do the rest.

- A common occurrence in some of these discussions is a person will **ask new questions as you are answering a previous question.** This creates a situation where the conversation goes around in circles.

- Make sure you reassure the person that you are willing to cover any questions they would like to ask, but you **want to focus on one subject, and question, at a time.**

- If a person is really wanting **to operate in a respectful, cooperative way**, this request will be honored. If a person is not willing to follow this guideline, they may not be open **to a healthy interaction of cooperation**.

- You want to stay friends with any person in your Bible study. **The best way to win a soul is to make a friend.** However, at some point, it may be time to simply part ways and simply pray for a person. Then find a new person who really wants to receive the Word.

- **The way I exit a potentially contentious interaction** is to say, "You keep doing what you're doing, and I'll do the same. If at any time what I'm doing isn't working for me, I will come to see you. If at any time what you're doing doesn't work for you, you come to see me."

- It is important to keep the right spirit in a biblical discussion. If the teacher steps out of the character of the Holy Ghost, the student is likely to not accept what the teacher is presenting because of how the teacher is acting. They tend to blame your behavior as the reason why what you are teaching is incorrect if it's different than what they have been taught previously.

- Then, the new convert will just stop coming to your Bible study, and you will **lose the opportunity** to be an influence in their lives and help them meet Jesus.

- **Never get into fight mode.** If it turns into an **ugly argument**, then this **is not edifying**. If either party has any issues with keeping the right spirit, **the study or discussion should end.** If both parties do things the appropriate way, another discussion in the future is much more likely. I believe this is the will of God.

- Present this Truth with knowledge, gentleness, humility, and love. **Know your material by studying it thoroughly.** The person **may not be ready** to receive the message today, but they will never come back to you tomorrow if the teacher is arrogant and full of pride.

- If you are operating in the Spirit according to **Galatians 5:22**, the Lord will inhabit your Bible study and wisdom and knowledge will be transferred to the student. **Galatians 5:22** *But the fruit of the Spirit* **is love, joy, peace, longsuffering, gentleness, goodness, faith, 23 Meekness, temperance:** *against such there is no law.*

- People are getting tired of churches that do not seem to match up with the scripture. Those people will be looking for the reason why. The KBS provides you with everything you need to show people that reason and guide them to what is missing from their relationship with Jesus.

- Not following these guidelines is another way to commit spiritual abortion. This is when a person is pushed too hard, too fast, which causes the person to not want God at all.

FINAL CONCLUSION

1. **Isaiah 28:13** But the word of the LORD **was unto them precept upon precept, precept upon precept; line upon line, line upon line; here a little,** [and] there a little; that they might go, and fall backward, and be broken, and snared, and taken. 14 Wherefore hear the word of the LORD, ye scornful men, that rule this people which [is] in Jerusalem.

   - The **Word of God is consistent** and does not contradict itself.

2. **Psalms 119: 89** For ever, O LORD, thy word is **settled** in heaven.

   - We need to be **determined, immovable, unwavering, and firm in our belief** in this **Truth**.

3. **1 Corinthians 15:1** Moreover, brethren, I declare unto you the **gospel** which I preached unto you, which also ye have received, and wherein **ye stand**; 2 By which also **ye are saved**, if ye keep in memory what I preached unto you, **unless ye have believed in vain**. 3 For I delivered unto you first of all that which I also received, how that **Christ died for our sins** according to the scriptures; 4 And that **he was buried**, and that **he rose again** the third day according to the scriptures:

   - Paul delivers the **Gospel**, which **we stand by**, and leads us to salvation.

   - **We MUST follow** what Paul preached, or our believing will be of no effect, and **our belief will be in vain.**

   - Paul states exactly what the Gospel is**; Jesus died** for our sins, **Jesus was buried** and **rose again on the third day. This is the death, burial, and resurrection.**

   - The way **WE enter** into the gospel of our salvation is to **die to sin** in repentance, **be buried** in water baptism (*submersion*), and the resurrection is the ability to **receive the Holy Ghost** (*Act 2:38*).

   - The Gospel, or good news, is that we have the opportunity to be saved, by obeying from the heart, what God commands. That is to be **born again** and then **walk in the Spirit** to **develop a holy life** (*Galatians 5:16*).

Trust the scriptures**, follow** instructions, and **find** the intimacy with God you have always been looking for. May this Bible study bless you and everyone you encounter. **Shine your light into the darkness of your communities.**

Every day we get closer and closer to the return of Jesus Christ. Everything you see going on, around the world, and in your own backyards, **tells you something biblical is happening**. The Kingdom Bible Study Series will get you, and the people you teach, **ready for the coming of the Lord. Don't be caught unaware but be prepared!**

Made in the USA
Columbia, SC
16 June 2024